BEAUTIFUL
BEAUFORT
by the Sea

Current and Upcoming Titles
In this Series

Beautiful Beaufort by the Sea, Guide to Beaufort, South Carolina. Definitive guidebook to this beloved historic waterfront town, now in its third edition.

Nantucket Island Guidebook. Continues the tradition of excellence in coastal guidebooks in this fresh look at the faraway island of Nantucket, Massachusetts.

Hilton Head Island Guidebook. The latest offering in our guidebook series covers everything you need to know about this popular resort island on the South Carolina coast.

BEAUTIFUL BEAUFORT
by the Sea

Guide
to
Beaufort,
South Carolina

George Graham Trask
Marie Bernice La Touche

Coastal Villages Press
Beaufort, South Carolina

Published by Coastal Villages Press, a division of
Coastal Villages, Inc., 2614 Boundary Street,
Beaufort, SC 29902, 803-524-0075.

Available at special discounts for bulk purchases
and sales promotions from the publisher
and your local bookseller.

ISBN 1-882943-02-3
Library of Congress Catalog Number: 93-074938

Third Edition, Third Printing
Printed in the United States of America

Acknowledgements

A GUIDEBOOK grows out of need and by accretion. This one began at the urging and by the hand of Marie Bernice La Touche, general manager during the years 1989-91 of Best Western Sea Island Inn in historic downtown Beaufort. The inn needed a way to inform its guests about what to see and where to dine in downtown Beaufort. My role was to approve and to edit the xeroxed handout.

When the supply was exhausted, I realized what was missing in our community was a guidebook, making reliable and comprehensive information about the area available to residents and visitors alike. A collaboration was born, a combination of Marie's inspiration, my determination, a great deal of hard work by both of us, and our triumph over the new technology of desktop publishing. The first edition of 48 pages appeared in 1992; the second edition of 72 pages in 1993; and now this third edition of more than 100 pages in 1994.

The reception the book has received proves the need. The accretion in the number of pages and in the scope of coverage reflects continuing growth in the size and popularity of the Beaufort area. It appears that this book is destined to continue through updates in the future.

A perfectionist, it is said, is one who tends to regard anything less than perfect as unacceptable. We offer this third edition as our current idea of the perfect guidebook to a small coastal town. Concepts of the perfect guidebook will no doubt change. One thing will not change: the perfection that is Beaufort.

Designed and edited by   George Graham Trask

Researched and written by   Marie Bernice La Touche
George Graham Trask

Special thanks to

Contributors   Rebecca Crowley
Nancy Deegan
Lise Ritsch
Lawrence Rowland
Constance Bowen Trask

Illustrator   David Anderson

Maps   George Graham Trask

Contents

Welcome to Beautiful Beaufort Queen of the Carolina Sea Islands

WELCOME to Beautiful Beaufort By The Sea, Queen of the Carolina Sea Islands. Because Beaufort is truly a crowning jewel with an extraordinary history that has been most carefully preserved, we have compiled information to help you make the most of Beaufort, whether you visit for a day or live here a lifetime.

Beaufort has been a destination for visitors and settlers for almost five centuries. Indeed, before that most transforming event called the Civil War, Beaufort was known far and wide as the "Newport of the South," a resort *par excellence*. Ever since, Beaufort has continued to boast of its ubiquitous waterfront situation, mild climate, tranquil landscapes, grand homes, gentle folks and welcoming hostelries.

Unlike almost everywhere else in the South, Beaufort escaped damage during the Civil War due to a momentous event in the very earliest months of the war. That cataclysm, known in these parts as the "Day of the Big Gun Shoot," happened on November 7, 1861, just a few months after the fall of Fort Sumter. A force of 30,000 Union troops invaded and occupied Beaufort. Warned of the invasion, every white Southerner fled for the duration of the war, four long years. Most never returned. Beaufort immediately became as thoroughly Union territory as the deepest reaches of Boston and New York.

The great houses here, originally built by wealthy rice and cotton planters in the days of the old South, became headquarters for the Union army in the Department of the South. Tens of thousands of soldiers from every Northern state were transported here by ship for bivouacking before moving out to battle. And the first great experiments in freedom for black people were carried out here beginning in early 1862, pointing the way to the Emancipation Proclamation and the 14th Amendment to the Constitution.

Ever since, Beaufort has been a peculiar place, an exquisite Southern town inhabited by Southerners and Northerners alike. The people of Beaufort today greet you in a spirit of pride for this old town and with a determination to retain its uniqueness. ❧

Beaufort Superlatives

P RIDE IN THE MANY outstanding features of Beaufort has been a hallmark of the people here for almost five centuries, and superlatives abound. Did you know that:

❦ Beaufort is located on an island called Port Royal Island. All of the surrounding land is also islands including Lady's Island, St. Helena Island, Fripp Island, Hunting Island, Dataw Island, Distant Island, Cat Island, Cane Island, Gibbes Island, Parris Island, Spring Island, Callawassie Island, Hilton Head Island, and Daufuskie Island. Altogether, there are hundreds of islands making up what are called the South Carolina Sea Islands.

❦ Until modern-day bridges were constructed, the only way to reach Beaufort and the surrounding islands was by boat. The first bridge to Lady's Island was not built until the 1920's and the bridge across Broad River toward Hilton Head Island and Savannah not until the 1950's.

❦ Beaufort was the site in 1514 of the second landing on the North American continent by Europeans. The first was the landing by Ponce De Leon and his men at St. Augustine, Florida, not far away from here and just one year earlier.

❦ Beaufort was the site in 1562 of the first Protestant settlement in North America, Jean Ribaut's French Huguenot settlement called Charlesfort.

❦ The town of Beaufort is the second oldest in South Carolina and among the oldest in the United States. Beaufort was chartered in 1711 as Beaufort Town. The only town in South Carolina established earlier is Charleston (known then as Charles Town), chartered in 1670.

❦ Before the Civil War (1861-1865), Beaufort was one of the wealthiest towns in the United States and was commonly regarded as the "Newport of the South" by wealthy planters who built grand summer homes here.

❦ Beaufort is one of a very few towns with its entire downtown designated a National Historic Landmark District. This is a result of the fact that Beaufort has perhaps more ante-bellum homes per block than any other town in America.

❦ In 1860 the first draft of the Ordinance of Secession from the Union was drawn up in a Beaufort house on Craven Street, now known as Secession House.

❦ In 1861, before any of the great battles of the Civil War, Beaufort was invaded by a great U.S. naval armada and occupied by Federal troops. The invasion was the largest in the history of the U.S. Navy until the Normandy. invasion in 1944.

❦ Beaufort was occupied by Union army troops throughout the Civil War. It served as Union army headquarters and a Union hospital zone for this region throughout the Civil War. As a result, Beaufort was virtually untouched by the battles, burning and destruction of war that so many other Southern towns experienced. This is one of the major reasons Beaufort is so well preserved today.

❦ Robert Smalls, a native Beaufortonian and Civil War hero, was one of the first black men to serve in the United States Congress.

❦ The Emancipation Proclamation, which freed the slaves in areas occupied by Federal troops during the Civil War, was first applied on January 1, 1863, to the only major occupied area: Beaufort and the surrounding Sea Islands.

❦ During the Civil War, Penn Normal School on St. Helena Island was founded by Quaker missionaries from Philadelphia as the first school for freed slaves in the United States. It remains today as a center of black culture, known as Penn Center. In the early 1960's Dr. Martin Luther King, Jr., and his staff made plans for his famous March On Washington at retreats on the Penn campus.

❦ After the Civil War Beaufort's economy was supported first by phosphate mining and then by large-scale truck farming. Thousands of acres produced fresh green vegetables, shipped to all parts of the nation. The soil here is some of the richest in the world and the climate affords a year-round growing season.

❧ Military bases have existed at Beaufort since the Civil War, and they have grown to become one of the area's most important industries. Three military installations call Beaufort their home: Marine Corps Recruit Depot Parris Island, Marine Corps Air Station Beaufort, and U.S. Naval Hospital Beaufort.

❧ In the 1950's, the growth of tourism began with the development of resorts on Hilton Head Island and Fripp Island. Since then numerous other islands in Beaufort County have been developed, and the entire county now enjoys a vigorous tourism and resort industry.

❧ In recent years a new and exciting movie-making industry has been introduced. Due to Beaufort's beauty, preservation and history, it has recently been the setting of major motion pictures, such as *Conrack, The Great Santini, The Big Chill, Glory, The Prince of Tides, Forrest Gump,* and *The War.*

❧ Beaufort has recently been "discovered" in a big way. Articles have appeared in almost all of the major national magazines and newspapers. For example, *The Sophisticated Traveler* section of a recent Sunday issue of *The New York Times* carried a feature article on London, Paris, Hong Kong and . . . Beaufort! *Vogue* magazine recently touted Beaufort in a feature article as "the South's hottest small town." And *Vogue* wasn't referring to the temperature. Beaufort is one of the "Top Ten Places To Live" according to *Outside* magazine.

All of this makes Beaufort special. What also makes Beaufort special is the friendliness of the people who live and work here. We know you'll find that almost everyone in Beaufort is quick with a smile and a "good day," so don't be surprised when you make some new friends. 🌿

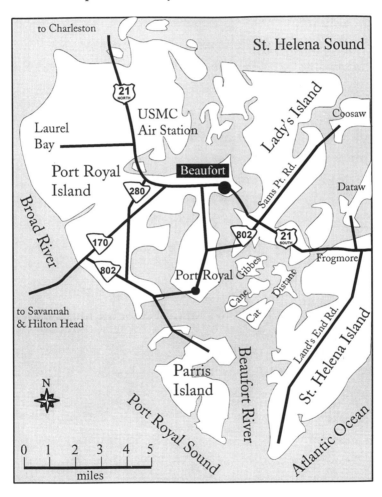

Special Beaufort Words

THERE ARE CERTAIN WORDS you cannot possibly be expected to know unless you've either lived here all your life or had someone explain them to you. Until you know these words, you will not understand what Beaufort is all about. We've decided to save you a lot of time and confusion by defining these words for you.

❦ **Beaufort**. You must, of course, start with the name of the town. The pronunciation has been the source of much confusion because the word looks as if it should be pronounced the French way, BO-FOR (rhymes with "go for"), or perhaps the North Carolina way, BO-FOOT (rhymes with "no foot"). Beaufort in the Loire Valley of France and Beaufort on the coast of North Carolina are lovely towns, but not our town and not our pronunciation. Here we say BEW-FOOT (starts like the first syllable in "beautiful").

A lovely lady from North Carolina tells the following story. The Duke of Beaufort in England is a noble title that still exists today. On a recent trip to Beaufort, North Carolina, the Duke of Beaufort was asked why South Carolinians pronounce the name of their town unconventionally. To which he replied, "My dear, because South Carolinians don't know how to talk."

Dr. Larry Rowland, noted historian of our fair town, told us that he had spoken with a professor of medieval

French who said that in the middle ages the French pronunciation of "beau" was BEW as in "beautiful," which would make our pronunciation correct. However, Dr. Rowland further pointed out that, though we are indeed tradition-bound, to assume our pronunciation is somehow linked to memory of medieval times may be stretching things a bit too far. He suggested that maybe the Duke of Beaufort was right after all.

Still others have suggested that our pronunciation, like our town, is linked visually to the word "beautiful," which would tend to fuel the embers of subtle rivalry between North and South Carolina. During the 18th century, North Carolina was commonly known as "poor Carolina" and South Carolina as "rich Carolina." North Carolina is still known by some as "the valley of humility between two mountains of conceit," referring to its neighboring states, South Carolina and Virginia.

Perhaps the most practical answer is simply that our pronunciation differs to distinguish our town in the minds of people who don't otherwise know the difference. Everywhere in this book we are referring to our town, Beautiful Beaufort By The Sea in South Carolina.

❦ **Beaufort Bay**. Although it is really just a wide spot in the Beaufort River, the Bay is known expansively as the waterway that goes roughly from Bellamy Curve where Boundary Street turns into Carteret Street southward all the way to the McTeer Bridge. More strictly, it is the downtown expanse of water over which Bay Street looks.

🦌 **Beaufort River**. Technically not a river, this is the large body of tidal water, part of the Atlantic Intracoastal Waterway, that runs from Port Royal Sound in the south up past the town of Beaufort in the direction of St. Helena Sound to the north. In the old days before the bridges connected these islands to the mainland, steamers ran in the Beaufort River to carry people and supplies to and from Savannah and Charleston. Tides run rapidly here, the normal variation from low to high tide being an extraordinary seven feet. Although the channel is very deep, there are sandbars scattered about. If your boat draws a lot of water, you'd better read the coastal charts, especially at low tide.

🦌 **Beaufort Salute**. The film crew for *The Great Santini* coined the term "Beaufort salute," though actually the recruits on Parris Island have been doing it as long as the rest of us. When the "no see ums" come out and you flick your hand over your face to shoo them away, that's the "Beaufort salute."

🦌 **Beaufort Style**. Now that Beaufort's become chic, our old homes have suddenly acquired their own "style," described at some length elsewhere in this book. We've always known that the old houses here overlooking the water with wide porches, raised basements and distinctive porticos were something special. If you're constructing or renovating a house on the water here, there's one especially important thing to remember: the front of your house is the side facing the water, no matter where the street is. Style has some other meanings in Beaufort, too. When you call the plumber because your sink is stopped up and he arrives three days later because he went fishing instead, he's "arriving in the Beaufort style." And when your friends in the city are running themselves ragged in the rat race of life and you're happy as a clam on a mud bank down here in Beaufort, you're "living in the Beaufort style."

🦌 **Dove Shoot**. One of God's greatest glories are mourning doves, beautiful migratory gray birds with the looks of small pigeons and a whistling in their wings when they fly. In springtime, they come here to mate on their way northward, sort of like Yankee folks sometimes do. Then in the fall they head back down far to the south, stopping off here for a rest and a snack on native seeds in woods and fields. For centuries Southern boys have lurked on the edge of the fields with shotgun ready, hoping beyond hope to fell one of these morsels to take home to mamma for supper. The dove have all of the advantages. In spring when the law prevents shooting them, they're as friendly as your neighborhood squirrel. But in the fall, when the sun gets low in the sky and you've been waiting in the field all afternoon, they suddenly dart out of the sun at two-hundred miles an hour, turning sideways flips just as you raise your trusty sixteen-gauge skyward, blinded by the glare. Fordham Hardware gets rich selling shotgun shells; the state of South Carolina gets rich selling shooting licenses; and good old boys enjoy a long, lazy afternoon in the great out of doors under the autumn sky.

🐸 **Frogmore**. Perhaps the word Frogmore is best described as a state of mind. Locals also know it as a reference to a crossroads on Highway 21 on St. Helena Island. The crossroads was linked to a nearby cotton plantation that was named for a royal palace in England. Improbably, the name stuck to the crossroads. Some folks around here have tried fervently to get rid of "Frogmore", but it keeps coming back, just like frogs do.

🐸 **Frogmore International Airport**. A tongue-in-cheek reference, coined by colorful local radio personality and raconteur Bill Peters, to our illustrious county airport located on Lady's Island, up the road from that croaking crossroads we told you about a minute ago. You can trust that no international flights land here. In fact, there is no commercial service at this airport. You may purchase T-shirts here though, with "Frogmore International" printed on them. Lady's Island Airport is the official name.

🐸 **Frogmore Stew**. This is a tasty combination of shrimp, sausage, corn on the cob, and onions with bay spice that is a local tradition. The name hails from Frogmore on St. Helena Island, presumably where the dish originated. We've been told it's so simple that even someone who can't boil an egg can make this stew. One thing's for sure, it's a whole lot better than a boiled egg. Here's the recipe for Frogmore's gift to mankind:

Frogmore Stew

This is the world's simplest gourmet feast. Serves approximately ten. Add more of everything to the water and seasoning if your guests haven't eaten in a week.

2 gallons water approximately
4 tablespoons Old Bay Seasoning or equivalent
1 medium onion chopped
2 pounds smoked sausage cut into 2-inch lengths
5 ears corn halved
3 pounds shrimp

Bring water to a boil in a large pot and add seasoning, onion, and sausage. Return to boil. Add corn and return to boil until done, about 15 minutes. Add shrimp, stirring often, until they turn just pink, about 4 minutes. Do not overcook the shrimp. Drain and serve with butter or cocktail sauce on table covered with newspaper for easy cleanup. Eat with your fingers and use paper towels like people in Frogmore do. Goes down well with cool beer. Mmmmmmmm, good!

🦐 **Gullah**. One of the prides of African-American culture is Gullah, a term that describes a geographical area centered on the Sea Islands surrounding Beaufort; cultural characteristics of the black people living on these islands; and their particular style of speech bordering on a separate language. Recent scholarship indicates that the Gullah's ancestors originated in Sierra Leone on the west coast of Africa. Brought here as slaves in the 18th century, they gained their independence in the earliest days of the Civil War as the result of the Federal invasion and occupation of the Sea Islands in 1861. The descendants of many of them have remained on these islands, carrying forward a strong culture and pride. Art, literature and scholarly works by and about the Gullah have brought a keen appreciation of their unique place in the American mosaic.

❦ **Live Oak**. Some folks are inclined to laugh when told that the beautiful trees they see draping over the river are "live oak," for the name would seem to identify the obvious. However, that's the real name of this tree, one of the very finest of the many varieties of oaks in the world, green leaves always present. And, as gorgeous as these trees are alive, with limbs reaching out three times as far as their towering height, they are equally valuable as timber, especially coveted by boat builders for strength and resistance to rot. The U.S. Navy's early sailing fleet was built entirely from live oak, "Old Ironsides" being probably the most famous testimonial to the tree's strength. When Hurricane Hugo came through South Carolina in September 1989 it uprooted many huge, old live oak trees, evidence of the incredible power of that storm. Sad as the uprooting was, it did have a positive result. Ship restorers collected fallen live oak timber from the storm and are using it to restore such historic sailing vessels as Mayflower II.

❦ **Lowcountry**. Geologically speaking, the state of South Carolina is divided into three regions, each with distinct terrain, climate and flora. The Piedmont or Upcountry is the upper part of the state at the foothills of the Appalachian mountains. The Sand Hills or Midlands are the middle part of the state with rolling sandy hills that were once coastal sand dunes. And the Lowcountry is the lower part of the state subject to the influence of the ocean and the tidal rivers and creeks leading to the ocean. Back millions of years ago during one of the periods of global warming, the ocean lapped on beaches far inland from here. When the ocean receded, the Lowcountry was revealed. Part of the Lowcountry is a series of islands, located primarily in Beaufort County, called the Sea Islands. When God made the Lowcountry, especially that part of it known as the Sea Islands, he called it paradise.

❦ **Marsh**. The verdant tidal pasture dividing the sea from the islands in our paradise is called marsh. It is the birthplace of much of the sea life and bird life in this part of our planet. In times past, much of the eastern coastline was covered in marsh, but the folly of man in the more industrialized states northward has caused much of its destruction. We have always been a gentler sort down here in the southland, closer to nature. No one dare destroy marsh here, and no one dare call it a swamp.

At a first glance, the marsh may not appear to be exciting. The more one lives with the ever-changing marsh, the more one falls in love with it. Watch the marsh change with the tides and the seasons. The marsh is never a still life picture. Whether the tide is coming in or going out, or the color of the grass is changing from green to gold, the marsh is always in flux. Have a picnic or spend a lifetime here; you'll see what we mean about the marsh.

🐾 **Oyster Roast**. Growing in the fertile tidal mud banks along the marsh is a succulent marine bivalve mollusk known as the oyster. For thousands of years, long before we white and black folks arrived from Europe and Africa, the Indians in these parts engaged in a peculiar ritual. They waded into the creek, reached down into the mud, pulled up the oyster, washed their shells in the cleansing salt water, spread them over a bed of hot coals with a moist covering on the river bank, then talked and laughed for about ten minutes. The result is roasted oysters, one of life's greatest culinary pleasures. Beaufort sophisticates today do exactly the same as the Indians, but usually arrive for the party in Weejuns and Madras and get somebody else to waddle around in the mud ahead of time. We moderns have bettered the Indians in one respect only: cool beer or white wine with which to wash down these delights. Cognoscenti bring their own gloves and oyster knives.

🐾 **Palmetto Tree**. Because of its name, some folks get the impression that this tree is not a true palm tree. Actually it is a palm tree through and through, growing as high as 60 feet and living as long as 75 years, but not producing coconuts the way its relatives in the tropics do. See them in formation at the Marine Corps Recruit Depot Parris Island, along the causeway. Not to be confused with "saw palmetto," a low shrub with thin, long fronds similar to palmetto leaves. Saw palmetto is also often confused with another local favorite, the yucca plant. The yucca with its beautiful white bloom is sometimes called "Spanish bayonet" because of its very sharp, pointed leaves. Truth to tell, when you start talking about palmetto trees you get into a complicated subject.

❦ **Sea Islands**. All of Beaufort County, with the exception of just a small portion on the mainland, is composed of islands, literally hundreds of them. If you fly over in an airplane, you will see water everywhere, interspersed with what appear to be sparkling jewels. The jewels are the islands. The sparkle is the water splashing against the marsh grass. This area has been called the Sea Islands ever since Europeans first set foot here almost five centuries ago. Isolated from the mainland far longer than almost any other area, many of these islands did not have bridges to them until the mid-20th century. Most do not directly face the ocean, but are on nearby tidal rivers, creeks and bays running to the ocean.

❦ **Spanish Moss**. That tangled, curly net draping from our live oaks (and other trees) is not just an ornamental conjuring up memories of the romantic old South. It is a favorite bedding for humans and animals alike. People use it as upholstery stuffing, and birds love to make their nests with it. Contrary to popular belief, this plant is not Spanish, is not a moss, and does not hurt its "host." It is an air plant that lacks interest in soil and so chooses to dangle freely from limbs to catch sunlight and rainwater. Botanically, Spanish moss is a member of the pineapple family. If you decide to take some home with you, be sure to put it in a tightly-sealed plastic bag. Heat the moss in your oven or microwave to kill the little red bugs. Otherwise, you'll be scratching!

🍍 **Tabby**. As the Indians feasted on oysters on the sand banks of their island paradise for eons, they tossed the spent oyster shells into big mounds. When the Europeans arrived, accustomed as they were to brick houses, they sought but found no clay here. So they invented tabby as a substitute. They dug the ancient oyster shells out of the Indian mounds, burned them over a big fire until they turned into powdered lime, stirred in whole oyster shells, sand and water, then poured this aggregate into wooden forms to create huge solid walls of tabby, a building material unique to this area.

🍍 **The Point**. When the folks at the British Colonial Office in London laid out the plan for the town of Beaufort in 1711, they chose the highest point of land on Port Royal Island that faces due south overlooking the water. That area today is the residential area of Bay Street. To the east was a low place, separated from the original town by a small, muddy creek. Over the years, the townspeople connected this point of low land to the town by filling the creek in with dirt. Venturesome settlers built small country houses there, and when some of them became filthy rich growing cotton in the mid-1800's, they built large mansions there. Today, this area is called the Point. And the point for some people is to live on the Point.

 Yankees. About 30,000 of this demonstrative race from up North, dressed in blue uniforms, staged a seaborne invasion here in November, 1861, and stayed throughout the Civil War. They and their descendants have been coming here as visitors and settlers ever since and seem to like this place. We've decided we like them too.

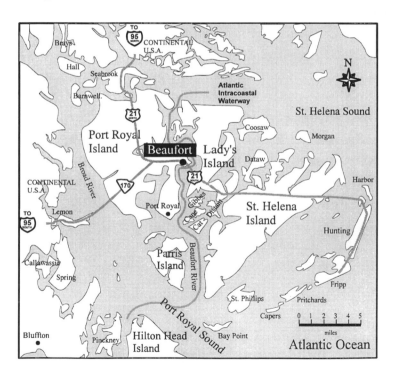

A Summary of Beaufort's History

BEAUFORT IS LOCATED on a large island near the confluence of a wide tidal sound with the Atlantic Ocean. Native American Indians inhabited this place for thousands of years before Europeans ever landed in the New World. The early European explorers called this entire area Port Royal. The island on which Beaufort is located is called Port Royal Island and the sound at the ocean's entrance is called Port Royal Sound. Across the sound is Hilton Head Island, also in Beaufort County.

Beaufort and the surrounding coastal areas to the south including St. Augustine, Florida, about 150 miles away, were among the first to be explored and settled in the New World. The Spanish, the French and the English were all interested in the area because of rich soil, abundant natural resources, and proximity to the West Indies which provided a viable trade route with Europe.

In 1514, the Spanish explored the Beaufort area under the leadership of Pedro De Salazar. In 1521, a Spanish fleet under the command of Francis Gordillo sailed into Port Royal Sound, surveyed the area and named it Punta de Santa Elena, which has since been anglicized to St. Helena. This name is now borne by St. Helena Island and St. Helena Sound, both in Beaufort County.

The Spanish fleet returned to Florida without establishing a settlement in this area. Then in 1562, Jean Ribaut, a French Huguenot, established a small settlement called Charlesfort almost within eyesight of what is now downtown Beaufort, the first Protestant settlement in North America. It was Ribaut who gave the name Port Royal to this area. The precise location of his settlement is not certain, though many people believe it to have been on the tip of Parris Island.

Whitsontide, Sunday, May 17, 1562

Being of the opynion that there was no fayrer or fytter place for the purpose then porte Royall, when we had sounded the entrey and the channell, (thanked be God) we entred salfely therin with our shippes agenst the opynyon of many, fynding the same one of the greatest and fayrest havens of the worlde . . . . In this porte are many armes of the sea depe and lardg, and here and there of all sides many rivers of a meane biggnes, where withowt danger all the shippes in the worlde myght be harbored.

—Jean Ribaut

Disease, lack of supplies, and the threat of attack by both Indians and the Spanish soon led the French colonists to abandon the settlement and its fortification. They sailed back across the Atlantic Ocean on a terrible journey that included casting lots to survive. Two years later the Spanish returned and established a settlement at Santa Elena that lasted 21 years. But Indian uprisings and French and English threats forced the Spanish to withdraw.

Without a significant Spanish presence, England was able to lay claim to this area in 1629. But it was not until 1670 that the English sent an expedition to Carolina. Under the leadership of William Sayle, this expedition came to Port Royal but did not settle here for fear of harassment by pirates and Spanish rovers based in nearby Florida. The English instead sailed north and founded Charles Town (Charleston), the first English settlement in South Carolina.

In 1685, a small band of Scottish Covenanters founded Stuart Town here. This colony was located just about a mile and a half from what is now downtown Beaufort, due south down the river. In 1686, the Spanish attacked and destroyed this Scottish settlement in retaliation for arming and inciting the Yemassee Indians against them.

The area finally became permanently settled when the English Crown decided to erect a seaport town here, named after the Duke of Beaufort. Beaufort was chartered in 1711, which makes it the second oldest town in South Carolina and among the earliest towns along the Eastern Seaboard.

With the chartering of Beaufort, the Anglican Church established St. Helena's Parish in 1712. In 1715 the nearby Yemassee Indians almost annihilated the settlers in the parish. The church building still stands today in downtown Beaufort, though only part of it is the original structure built in 1726 after the threat of the Indians subsided.

Principal industries in Beaufort during colonial days

were rice and indigo. Indigo was valued for its use as a textile dye, which in those days was fast becoming a booming industry in Europe. The darker the blue in the indigo dye, the more valuable it was on the market. With these cultivated resources, Beaufort began to prosper.

Thomas Heyward, whose plantation was located near Beaufort, was a leading South Carolina patriot and one of the signers of the *Declaration of Independence*. During the Revolution Beaufort was occupied by British troops, and some British soldiers from this war are buried in St. Helena's graveyard.

After the American Revolution, Beaufort continued as an established town in its own right, without formal ties to England. The development of cotton plantations introduced a new source of prosperity for the area. Beaufort became renowned for its long-staple Sea Island cotton, which was considered the finest cotton in the world.

During this period leading up to the Civil War, Beaufort experienced tremendous growth and wealth. Many of the houses were built during this time (1786-1860) as summer homes for wealthy plantation owners who wished to escape the heat and the risk of malaria inland. Because Beaufort was on the water and had a southerly exposure, it was cooler and less susceptible to mosquitoes than the inland areas where rice and cotton plantations were located. Grand parties and gatherings were an expression of these prosperous times, and homes were built then for entertaining as much as for living.

Beaufort was home for a number of South Carolina's states' rights firebrands. The first Ordinance of Secession from the Union was drawn up in 1860 in what is now known as Secession House, located on Craven Street. Robert Barnwell Rhett, a Beaufortonian, was especially instrumental in facilitating this Ordinance. In other words, secession from the Union, which proved disastrous to the South, began right here in Beaufort.

The war began in April 1861 with the Rebels shelling Fort Sumter in Charleston harbor. To wage war against the South, the Union needed a secure port, bivouac area and coaling station on the South Atlantic coast. For these purposes almost 30,000 Union troops invaded Beaufort by sea in November 1861 and occupied this area throughout the war. Immediately before the invasion, almost every white person fled the area, never to return. Most took only necessities and left their homes almost entirely intact. They also left behind almost 10,000 slaves on their Sea Island plantations.

Union troops took over the homes and churches, and Beaufort served as a hospital zone and Union army headquarters throughout the war. St. Helena's Episcopal Church and the Baptist Church of Beaufort both served as hospitals. Tombstones at St. Helena's Church were used as operating tables. Injured Union soldiers were brought to Beaufort because it was safe territory and easily accessible by sea.

Many of the houses in the downtown historic district also served as hospitals. The John Mark Verdier House on Bay Street (now a house museum open to the public) served as the Union army headquarters building. Because battles were not waged in Beaufort, the town was spared the destruction that many other Southern towns saw during the war. And General Sherman smiled broadly on Beaufort because, rather than engaging in his usual incendiary habits, he merely took a boat ride over from Savannah after his march through Georgia to visit his Union army friends headquartered here. General Sherman spent the night in Beaufort before embarking with the Union troops encamped here on his ruinous campaign through rebellious South Carolina.

Beaufort, June 6, 1863

Dear Mother, This is an odd sort of place. All the original inhabitants are gone—and the houses are occupied by Northerners.

Your loving son,

Robert Gould Shaw

Because of the Federal occupation of Beaufort throughout the Civil War, many Northern civilians came here then, and many of them loved this area so much that they stayed for the remainder of their lives. Beaufort has been justly proud of its Yankee inhabitants ever since, and many of them continue to come here to live permanently.

During the Civil War occupation, the U. S. Government imposed a Federal real estate tax on the land and homes here. The Southern owners being absent and unable to pay the tax, the land was confiscated. The homes in town were auctioned to Union soldiers and civilians, and the plantations were cut into 40-acre tracts and sold for nominal sums to the newly freed slaves. In 1862, Penn Normal School was established as a trade school for these freedmen on St. Helena Island, teaching them how to work as independent farmers on the land they had acquired. As a result, black residents in Beaufort County became landowning small farmers, not tenant farmers. The campus of their first school, now called Penn Center, is still in existence today and is open to the public.

St. Helenaville, Thursday, November 17, 1864

[Penn] school flourishing, household matters comfortable, living good, and all things smooth at present . . . . We have a very large school and a charming time in it. Just think, you poor, freezing, wind-pierced mortals! *We* have summer weather. The fields are gay with white, purple, and yellow flowers, and with the red leaves of sumach and other shrubs. Our woods are always green, and just now the gum trees make them beautiful with red. *You* can't see a leaf! Chill November! I pity you.

—Laura M. Towne

During the period following the war, Beaufort's population was largely black, outnumbering whites seven to one. Robert Smalls, a Beaufortonian who had been a slave and then a Civil War hero to the Union, became one of the first black U. S. Congressmen and served a long and prominent political career. A statue on Craven Street next to Tabernacle Baptist Church commemorates his contributions.

With the establishment of a U.S. Naval Station on Parris Island in 1891, Beaufort began to experience the role the military would play in its future. The installation subsequently became the Marine Corps Recruit Depot Parris Island. In 1942, a U.S. Naval Air Station was established in the Gray's Hill area near Beaufort, on land that became the Marine Corps Air Station Beaufort. These bases, together with the U.S. Naval Hospital, support the economy and growth Beaufort enjoys today. In addition to active-duty military families living here, many retired military people love Beaufort so much that they have chosen it as their permanent home.

During the twentieth century, especially in the middle decades, truck farming became a major part of the economy. Large farms on Port Royal Island, St. Helena Island, Cane Island, Cat Island, and Distant Island produced as many as thirty-five different varieties of fresh vegetables in three seasons annually, summer being the only time when the weather was too hot for growing vegetables commercially. Truck farming has continued, especially tomatoes, but not nearly to the extent of prior decades. Commercial fishing and shrimping also became a part of Beaufort's economy, but they too appear to be on the wane.

In recent years retirement communities and tourism have become vital parts of the economy, though Beaufort seeks vigilantly to maintain its small-town ambiance in order to avoid over-commercialization.

A fledgling film industry began with the filming here of *The Great Santini* in the late 1970's and *The Big Chill* in the early 1980's. Tom Berenger, who starred in *The Big Chill*, liked Beaufort so much that he decided to make it his permanent home. In the summer of 1990 film crews making *The Prince of Tides* were in town for seven months, including the stars Barbra Streisand and Nick Nolte. In 1993, the town hosted the making of two more major films, *Forrest Gump* and *The War*, whose stars, Tom Hanks, Sally Fields, and Kevin Costner, could often be seen strolling about town.

All the while the people of Beaufort have gone about their business as usual, the way they have around here for almost five-hundred years. 🌿

A Tour of Beaufort's Historic District

BEAUFORT IS A TOWN ON AN ISLAND, and the town is defined by its proximity to the sea. The downtown historic district encompasses the boundaries of the old town, focused on the waterfront facing due south. Some of the houses date back to the early 1700's, and almost all of them have outstanding architectural features.

The best way to see old Beaufort is by strolling. The historic district is relatively small and easily traversed on foot. If you would like a personally guided walking tour, check at the Greater Beaufort Visitors' Center; guides usually charge about $10.00 per hour. Or you may wish to see the old parts of town on a bicycle, available for rent at the Greater Beaufort Chamber of Commerce Visitors' Center, at Best Western Sea Island Inn (1015 Bay Street), and at Lowcountry Bicycles (904 Port Republic Street). A particularly fun way is the Horse-Drawn Carriage Tour with its leisurely pace and knowledgeable guides. Purchase your tickets at the Chamber of Commerce Visi-

tors' Center, located on the waterfront at the foot of the waterfront park and downtown marina. The Point Tours are conducted in minibuses and cater to the special interests of tourists, covering such places as antique shops and tea rooms. The tours leave on the hour and can be booked at the Greater Beaufort Chamber of Commerce Visitors' Center.

Be sure to take enough time to savor the ambiance. Stroll or ride in front of the grand houses on Bay Street facing due south on the high bluff; explore the Point to the east with its narrow side streets running to the water. In between is the downtown shopping district with lots of specialty shops, restaurants and the beautiful waterfront park.

PUBLIC BUILDINGS

Greater Beaufort Chamber of Commerce Visitors' Center, 1006 Bay Street, 524-3163. At the western end of the waterfront park near the downtown marina, the Visitors' Center is the place for visitors and residents to begin their tour of historic Beaufort. Tour maps, tour books, information about community events, promotions of local businesses, friendly and knowledgeable staff, and tickets for carriage and boat tours are just a few of the benefits of a visit here. Open daily and Sundays.

Henry C. Chambers Waterfront Park, on the bay in beautiful downtown Beaufort. This lovely public park with a fabulous view looking south over the bay was designed by renowned landscape architect Robert Marvin. The park has picnic areas, a seasonal farmer's market on Saturdays, and a covered pavilion which features concerts, art shows and local events. There is also a large playground for children and swings on the waterfront for their parents to take in the views as well. Not to be missed. Concerts and other special events are a feature of the waterfront park. Schedules are available at most of the downtown shops and at the Greater Beaufort Chamber of Commerce Visitors' Center, 1006 Bay Street. Enter the park from Bay Street at the Visitors' Center, through a landscaped walkway next to The Gadsby Tavern, or at the foot of the Lady's Island Bridge. Parking is available nearby.

🌱 **St. Helena's Episcopal Church, 507 Newcastle Street, 522-1712,** parish established 1712, bounded by North, Church, King and Newcastle Streets. Seat of one of the earliest parishes established in the New World, this church is steeped in history and is beautifully restored. Only a small portion of the building itself is original (1724)

because the church was expanded over the years to meet the needs of the increasing congregation. The structure you see today was essentially complete no later than the mid-1800's. The graveyard is well worth walking through; it is filled with gravestones reaching back in time. A guidebook to the history and anecdotes about the gravestones can be purchased from the parish office located on Newcastle

Street. The tombstones were used during the Civil War as operating tables. The church building and the graveyard are open to the public and guided tours are also available. Well-trained docents are stationed inside the church to tell you about its history.

❦ **The Baptist Church of Beaufort, 600 Charles Street, 524-3197.** This stately Greek Revival structure was constructed in 1844, under the ministry of the great Dr. Richard Fuller. A Beaufort native, he became a nationally famous Baptist minister and helped to found the Southern Baptist Convention. Much of the original structure is still intact, though during the Civil War pews were removed and scattered so that the church could serve as a hospital. Miraculously, the pews were recovered and restored, as was the communion table, and are used today. Then, in 1959, Hurricane Gracie blew the roof off. Incredibly, the ornamental ceiling, which is 98% original, was not damaged. The tall steeple on the church, which can be seen from miles away and has become a symbol of Beaufort, was erected in 1961. The church is open to the public for viewing as well as worship. Friendly, knowledgeable docents are available to give you a tour of the church and tell you about its history, Mondays through Saturdays.

❦ **John Mark Verdier House, 801 Bay Street, 524-6334.** A house museum open to the public, this structure is meticulously restored and maintained by Historic Beaufort Foundation. Built about 1790 by Beaufort's merchant prince, John Mark Verdier, soon after the end of the Revolutionary War, it displays antiques from the Federal period, some of which belonged to Verdier himself. General Lafayette spoke from the front steps in 1825. The house served as Union army headquarters in the Civil War. Allow about 45 minutes to tour. Also, there is a gift shop with cards, books and gifts from Beaufort. Brochures and schedules on this house tour are available at the Greater Beaufort Chamber of Commerce Visitors' Center.

🐌 **The Arsenal, 713 Craven Street, 525-7471.** Originally constructed (1795-1852) to quarter the Beaufort Volunteer Artillery, one of the oldest military units in the United States, this castellated military structure now houses a small museum. Muskets, machine guns, grenades, and stuffed animal heads make up some of its treasures. Of unusual interest is its display of some of the insects that inhabited this region before pesticides came along—you simply will be amazed at the sight of some of these (not for the faint-hearted). The museum is currently undergoing a thorough revamping, so you'd better hurry if you want to see what has fondly become known as Beaufort's "attic"; before too long it may look like just another museum. Outside, the building has been freshened up with a yellow lime wash, a historical reference that has brought lightness and cheer to this part of Craven Street. This museum charges a small admission fee, but appears on most occasions to accept much-needed donations.

Beautiful Beaufort by the Sea

Copyright ©1994, Coastal Villages, Inc.

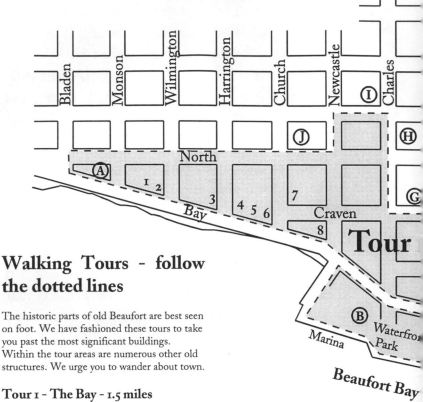

Walking Tours - follow the dotted lines

The historic parts of old Beaufort are best seen on foot. We have fashioned these tours to take you past the most significant buildings. Within the tour areas are numerous other old structures. We urge you to wander about town.

Tour 1 - The Bay - 1.5 miles

This is the original part of old Beaufort, chartered in 1711 by act of the British Crown. Centered on Bay Street along the waterfront, it includes the downtown shopping district, historic churches, and magnificent houses on the Bay facing due south.

Tour 2 - The Point - 1.5 miles

This is the "new" part of old Beaufort, an extension of the earliest neighborhoods. It contains grand old houses on narrow streets running to the water.

Tour 3 - Waterfront Park - 1/2 mile

Beaufort was originally accessible only by water. The waterfront park stands on the site of the old downtown docks and wharves.

Public Buildings:

A. U.S. Courthouse (under renovation)
B. Chamber of Commerce
C. Verdier House Museum (Historic Beaufort Foundation), c. 1790
D. City Hall
E. Public Library
F. Arsenal Museum, 1795
G. Tabernacle Baptist Church, c. 1840
H. U.S. Post Office
I. Baptist Church of Beaufort, 1844
J. St. Helena's Episcopal Church, 1724
K. Performing Arts Center
L. Univ. of S.C. at Beaufort campus (Beaufort College, 1852)
M. St. Peter's Catholic Church, 1846
N. First African Baptist Church, 1865

Greene

22

Washington

Duke

Prince

Scotts

King

North

Carteret

Republic

Bay

Tour 3

(K)

(L)

21

Baynard

(M)

Hancock

Hamilton

(N) 23

East

New

Laurens

15

Pinckney

19

18

16

17

Short

King

Tour 2

Federal

14

13

11

(F)

12

(E)

(D)

(C)

10

9

The Point

N

9. Lewis Reeve Sams House, 1852, 601 Bay St.
10. Thomas Hepworth House, c. 1717, 214 New St.
11. *The Castle,* Joseph Johnson House, c. 1850, 411 Craven St.
12. Henry Farmer House, c. 1810, 412 East St.
13. *Tidewater,* William Fripp House, c. 1830, 302 Federal St.
14. *Marshlands,* James Robert Verdier House, c. 1814, 501 Pinckney St.
15. Edward Means House, c. 1853, 604 Pinckney St.
16. The Green, a private park
17. *The Oaks,* Paul Hamilton House, c. 1856, 100 Laurens St.
18. *Big Chill House* or *Tidalholm,* Edgar Fripp House, c. 1856, 1 Laurens St.
19. Berners Barnwell Sams House No. 2, 1852, 201 Laurens St.
20. *Riverview,* Elizabeth Hext House, c. 1720, 207 Hancock St.
21. Rev. Thomas E. Ledbetter House, early 1800's, 411 Baynard St.
22. Elizabeth Barnwell Gough House, c. 1789, 705 Washington St.
23. William Wigg Barnwell House, c. 1816, 501 King St.

Private Homes (not open to public):

Edward Barnwell House, 1785, 1405 Bay St.
John Joyner Smith House, c. 1811, 400 Wilmington St.
Leverett House, pre-Revolutionary, 1301 Bay St.
Tabby Manse, Thomas Fuller House, c. 1786, 1211 Bay St.
Robert Means House, c. 1790, 1207 Bay St.
John A. Cuthbert House, c. 1810, 1203 Bay St.
Secession House, Milton Maxcy House, c. 1813, 1113 Craven St.
The Anchorage, William Elliott House, pre-Revolutionary, 1103 Bay St.

PRIVATE HOMES

The oldest neighborhoods in Beaufort, on the Bay and the Point, compose a collection of some the most outstanding early residences in America. All of the old houses face due south in order to catch the cooling sea breezes in summer and the warming southern sun in winter. The relationship of the house to the street does not determine its front; the front always faces south. Almost all of the houses are built on a raised basement. Many have rear wings projecting in a T pattern to allow back rooms a breeze and view of the water. These features, together with expansive porches across the fronts and in some cases wrapping around the sides, have come together in a most pleasant way to be known as the "Beaufort style."

1. Edward Barnwell House, 1785, 1405 Bay Street. Lovely interior paneling and mantels. Barnwell dynasty founded by "Tuscarora Jack" Barnwell, famous 18th-century Indian fighter who came here from Ireland. Union officers' quarters during Civil War.

2. John Joyner Smith House, c. 1811, 400 Wilmington Street. Massive columns create wonderful porches, ornate false front door facing Bay Street, south in the proper "Beaufort style." Drawing rooms across entire front. Generals' quarters and hospital during Civil War.

3. Leverett House, pre-Revolutionary, 1301 Bay

Street. Originally a plantation house on St. Helena Island, moved here by boat around 1850. Grand views from porch, close by water.

4. Thomas Fuller House, *Tabby Manse*, **c. 1786, 1211 Bay Street.** Beloved architectural gem and prototype of houses in the "Beaufort style." Delicate portico, solid tabby walls, exceptional interior. Built as wedding gift for bride, Elizabeth Middleton. Her first cousin, Arthur Middleton,

signed *Declaration of Independence.* Francis Griswold wrote *A Sea Island Lady* while staying here, describing Tabby Manse as "the heart" of the house he called Marshlands.

5. Robert Means House, c. 1790, 1207 Bay Street. Lovely drawing rooms and mantels, built after Revolutionary War by prominent merchant and planter. Home of U.S. Secretary of Navy Edwin Denby during 1920's.

6. John A. Cuthbert House, c. 1810, 1203 Bay Street. Strong classical exterior, numerous Victorian additions. Residence of Union General Rufus Saxton during Civil War, visited by his friend General William Tecumseh Sherman in early 1865 just before Sherman's infamous march northward through South Carolina.

7. Milton Maxcy House, *Secession House*, **c. 1813, 1113 Craven Street.** Magnificent Greek Revival exterior, arcaded basement, marble staircase, ornate ironwork. South Carolina's Ordinance of Secession from Union first drafted here. Union soldiers' graffiti on basement walls.

8. William Elliott House, *The Anchorage,* **pre-Revolutionary, 1103 Bay Street.** Elliott family owned Parris Island before Civil War. Originally a tabby house, massively changed by Admiral Beardsley in early 1900's.

9. Lewis Reeve Sams House, 1852, 601 Bay Street. Handsome mid-18th century "Beaufort style" house, Doric and Ionic columns, marble steps. From the porches there is the feeling of being on the prow of a boat on the water.

10. Thomas Hepworth House, c. 1717, 214 New Street. Beaufort's oldest house, with musket slits to ward off Indians in north wall of raised basement. Dutch colonial architecture, built by chief justice of colony.

11. Joseph Johnson House, *The Castle,* **c. 1850, 411 Craven Street.** One of most photographed houses in America. Grand mansion, massive oaks, overlooks bend in river. Solid brick walls, exterior and interior. Accomplished horticulturist, Dr. Johnson, planted original gardens.

12. Henry Farmer House, c. 1810, 412 East Street. Broad pedimented portico, fine interior. Residence of Dr. Richard Fuller, nationally famous Baptist leader before and after Civil War, whose wife owned Cat Island.

13. William Fripp House, *Tidewater,* **c. 1830, 302 Fripp Street.** On river set back from street. Built by "Good Billy" Fripp, still remembered for his generosity and goodness.

14. James Robert Verdier House, *Marshlands,* **c. 1814, 501 Pinckney Street.** Marvelous Caribbean-style exterior with one-story porch around three sides, beautiful Adam-style interior. Headquarters of U.S. Sanitary Commission during Civil War. Adopted the name Marshlands after the house of that name in *A Sea Island Lady.*

15. Edward Means House, c. 1853, 604 Pinckney Street. Beautiful brick mansion, facing south as do all old Beaufort houses, but front door at side like John Joyner Smith House (2). Graceful spiral staircase inside.

16. The Green, a private park encompassing an entire city block, helping to make old Beaufort an especially wonderful place.

17. Paul Hamilton House, *The Oaks,* **c. 1856, 100 Laurens Street.** Large oaks surround grand verandahs. Built by grandson of President James Madison's Secretary of the Navy; roof walk similar to mansions on Nantucket Island, Massachusetts.

18. Edgar Fripp House, *Tidalholm,* **c. 1856, 1 Laurens Street.** At tip of the Point, water on three sides. Built as summer home, saved from Civil War auction by generous Frenchman. *The Big Chill* and *The Great Santini* filmed here.

19. Berners Barnwell Sams House No. 2, 1852, 201 Laurens Street. Serene brick Classical Revival mansion facing the Green (16). Dependencies include blacksmith, cookhouse, laundry, storeroom, servants' quarters.

20. Elizabeth Hext House, *Riverview,* **c. 1720, 207 Hancock Street.** In countryside out of town when built, a small, intimate house on a large lot on the river. Elizabeth's husband, William Sams, owned Dataw Island.

21. Reverend Thomas E. Ledbetter House, early 1800's, 411 Baynard Street. A large, beautiful country house on a large lot on the river. Clara Barton, founder of American Red Cross, came here after 1893 hurricane.

22. Elizabeth Barnwell Gough House, c. 1789, 705 Washington Street. Twin of Tabby Manse (4), different portico and interior details. Downstairs paneling removed 1930's, found in California fifty years later, reinstalled. Tempestuous Elizabeth's grandson, Robert Barnwell Rhett, was "Father of Secession."

23. William Wigg Barnwell House, c. 1816, 501 King Street. Three-story mansion, built by grandson of Revolutionary War hero, Major William Hazzard Wigg. Saved from destruction and moved three blocks to this site in 1970's by Historic Beaufort Foundation. ❧

Other Major Points of Interest

N EAR THE DOWNTOWN historic district are a number of other major points of interest. Most are just a few blocks or a few short miles away, easily reached by car in a few minutes:

❦ **National Cemetery**, intersection of Bladen and Boundary Streets, just outside the downtown historic district. This cemetery dates back to 1863 when it was established as one of twelve national cemeteries by President Abraham Lincoln. Most of those buried here are Union soldiers from the Civil War. This is a beautiful, tranquil place with massive old live oaks and magnolia trees. Each year on Memorial Day (called Decoration Day here), the graves are decorated and a memorial service is held in memory of the war dead of our nation.

❦ **Marine Corps Recruit Depot Parris Island**, five miles south of downtown Beaufort. Parris Island sits in view over the water in the distance as you stand looking south on the high bluff on Bay Street. To reach Parris Island, take Bay Street onto Ribaut Road and follow the signs south to the Parris Island gate.

This depot began as a naval station with a small detachment of Marines in 1891. It has grown to become the main recruit training station for the United States Marine Corps. Almost the entire depot is open to the public. Graduation of recruits each Friday morning is awe inspiring. Sword drills and parade marches performed to perfection, with stirring music by the Marine Corps Band, make up the 90-minute ceremony. Guaranteed to rekindle patriotic fires. Call the Douglas Visitors' Center on the base at 525-3650 for more information.

The Parris Island depot is located on historic ground indeed. French Huguenots landed here in 1562, and the Spanish built the fort of Santa Elena four years later. These sites can be reached by car and observed up close on foot. Several archaeological digs have been performed here, as well as re-enactments of the French and Spanish landings. Be sure to check in April or May if the dig is going on; the archaeologists enjoy giving tours. If you have the time and inclination, you can help them.

🦌 **Parris Island Museum, 525-2951,** is a source of information not only for the depot, but military history as well. This museum is spit-polished, as you might expect, and is expertly curated. Plan to spend some time here if you're a military buff. Also of note on Parris Island is the inspirational Iwo Jima Monument, located near the parade deck, which was the original prototype for the more renowned monument erected later in Washington, D.C.

🦌 **Old Sheldon Church Ruins**, about a half-hour's drive from downtown Beaufort. These impressive ruins are all that remain of Prince William's Parish Church built between 1745-55. The original church was burned by British troops during the Revolutionary War and was rebuilt in 1825, only to be burned again by Sherman's troops in their march across South Carolina late in the Civil War. Architecturally, the church was conceived as a Greek temple, the first Greek Revival structure in the United States, and its large columns still stand today. Take Highway 21 north to the intersection with Highway 17 at Gardens Corner, bear left at the intersection, go about 500 yards, turn right onto Secondary Road 21 and follow the signs to Sheldon Church.

❦ **Penn Center**, St. Helena Island. This campus, established in 1862 by Quakers from Philadelphia, is particularly historic and beautiful. There is a museum of black history with artifacts, sweetgrass baskets, weavings, historical books, and photographs of students from Penn Normal School. This school, established during the Civil War, is world renowned for being the first school for freed slaves following emancipation, and the campus continues today to offer special programs. The late Dr. Martin Luther King, Jr., used this campus as a retreat and planned his famous March On Washington here. Go across the downtown bridge straight ahead on Highway 21 south to Frogmore on St. Helena Island, then turn right onto Lands End Road and drive about a mile.

❦ **Chapel of Ease**, on Lands End Road on St. Helena Island about a mile past the Penn Center campus. The remains of this church, built of tabby and brick, still stand today following damage by fire in 1886. The church was built in 1740 to serve planters living on the outlying

Sea Islands, thus the name Chapel of Ease for its convenient location.

❦ **Fort Fremont,** at Lands End on St. Helena Island. This fort facing the sea was built during the Spanish-American War to guard the entrance to Port Royal Sound. Remains of the hospital building and concrete gun emplacements still stand, but beware of ghosts. A very famous ghost, who is rumored to be a soldier who lost his head, is said to lurk here at night. The ghost carries a lantern, which appears as a mysterious light, as he searches the grounds for his head. Go several miles past Penn Center and the Chapel of Ease to the end of Lands End Road.

❦ **Hunting Island State Park, 838-2011.** This public beach and ocean-front park is about a twenty-minute drive from downtown Beaufort. Take Highway 21 south over the downtown bridge and continue across Lady's Island, St. Helena Island and a number of bridges until you arrive on Hunting Island at the park entrance. Miles of beaches, which are unusually wide at low tide, are available for walking, sunning, running and generally playing. Shell collecting is a favorite pastime here. However, please take only empty shells and dead sand dollars so future generations can enjoy this pastime too. Small waves and shallow water make Hunting Island an ideal outing for children. Rest rooms and vending facilities are available, though no lifeguards are present.

There are also nature trails which wind through the

subtropical landscape. The plant life in this park is un-usually dramatic and beautiful. Check with the Hunting Island Visitors' Center (follow signs at entrance to park) for trail information.

A marsh boardwalk on the side of Hunting Island op-posite the ocean is part of the park. This is a nature walk literally through the marsh. Be sure to look in the marsh carefully for crabs and birds—there is teeming life here.

🦟 **Hunting Island Lighthouse.** Located in the Hunt-ing Island State Park on the north end of the beach, the

lighthouse is open to the public to enjoy the spectacular view it pro-vides. Take a left following the signs to the north beach; it is a long and twisty road. The lighthouse was first established in 1859, but was rebuilt in 1860 due to beach ero-sion. In 1889 it had to be relocated again due to beach erosion. It was an active lighthouse until 1933. 🌿

Flora and Fauna of the Sea Islands

OUR VERDANT FORESTS and lush marshes have an abundance of flora and fauna all their own. We have already mentioned a few in our chapter "Special Beaufort Words." Here are some other interesting creatures you will meet if you keep your eyes peeled:

🌱 **Alligator.** Depending on your curiosity and fortitude, you may or may not want to encounter this reptile. Alligators live in our freshwater ponds, not in the ocean or the saltwater creeks. They can grow up to 15 feet in length, weighing 500 pounds. Smaller than crocodiles (which are found in Africa, not here), they can be distinguished by wide, flat snouts. In winter they hibernate in underground dens, appearing again in March. You can safely observe them from the bridge over the pond at Hunting Island State Park, though you may have to search the water carefully, for they are masters of disguise. Respect this fascinating reptile; *never* try to feed one. It will charge and can outrun you for 50 yards. If you find yourself in this most unfortunate predicament, retreat rapidly in a zig-zig pattern; alligators have trouble turning quickly while running. Errant golfer's tip: don't try to save money by retrieving your ball out of a pond unless you want to become an alligator's dinner. And be careful if you have a dog. 'Gators eat dogs for hors d'oeuvres.

❦ **Atlantic Blue Crab.** A delicacy in the South, blue crabs thrive in our tidal waterways and appear on most of the menus in our local restaurants. Those floating bottles and balls you see in the waterways mark crab traps made of wire mesh. Don't rob the traps. They are somebody's livelihood, and local fishermen guard them with some degree of ferocity. Instead, get a chicken neck, tie it to a string, and throw it into the water off any dock. When you feel a tug, pull slowly; up will come a crab. Keep only crabs that are five inches or larger across the shell. Throw back all females with eggs.

❦ **Azalea.** Spring hasn't totally sprung in Beaufort until the azaleas come into bloom in late March or early April. The brilliant flowers on these shrubs come in colors of fuschia, salmon, crimson, orange and white, and can be found in just about everyone's garden here. The traditional *indica* varieties are the large azaleas with the abundance of blooms.

❦ **Bottle-nosed Dolphin.** Most folks think these playful mammals, often called porpoise here, inhabit only ocean waters, but dolphins love to cruise our inshore tidal waterways too. Highly social animals, they are usually found in small schools of four to six. You may see them around fishing boats, either playfully swimming along-side, or hoping for a free bite or two. Also look for them at the beach, surfing the ocean waves. Local lore records an albino dolphin that was captured and taken to Florida. As a result, the South Carolina State Legislature has out-lawed the capture of dolphins for aquatic display.

❦ **Cordgrass or Spartina.** This is the dominant tall grass of the marsh, growing to six feet in height. Cordgrass bakes in the mud at temperatures up to 140 degrees at low tide, then endures inundation by salt water as the tide rises, all the while looking like a robust field of wheat. Would that front lawns were so hardy.

❦ **Fiddler Crab.** These crabs are too small for eating, but they sure can fiddle. Look for them among the dead cordgrass that washes ashore along tidal flats at low tide. You'll recognize them immediately with their single, over-sized claw (male only), which they use as a weapon and for feeding. They also use their "fiddle" for courting fe-males—just a wave and the girls come running.

❦ **Ghost Crab.** These little crabs come out only at night, worth your effort to observe them. Grab a flash-light and explore the beach after dusk. Look carefully and you'll see ghost crabs by the dozens. Beige in color, they blend with the sand, hence their name since they seem to vanish before your very eyes. The name may also come from the fact that they move so quickly that it's a case of "now you see them, now you don't."

❦ **Loggerhead Sea Turtle.** Count yourself lucky should you witness a loggerhead sea turtle. These wondrous creatures face harrowing circumstances in the cycle of life. Between May and August females drag their 350-pound bodies up the beach at an excruciatingly slow pace; dig a nest for hours with their giant flippers to lay about 150 eggs; then another couple of hours kick sand back over the nest, finally dragging themselves back down the beach to the sea. Two months later, if the nest has been undisturbed by raccoons, crabs and people, hatchlings emerge and scamper to the beach, vulnerable to preying birds. Once in the sea, the young turtles face fish whose favorite dish is turtle soup. Virtually 99.9 % percent of the young don't make it to adulthood. The ones that do are rewarded with lives of a hundred years or more. If you spot a loggerhead nest, *do not* disturb it in any way, but report immediately to the park ranger or the local turtle protection project. Never shine a light on loggerhead turtles, and keep lights around beach houses to a minimum. Help us protect our precious turtles.

❦ **Magnolia.** You can find magnolias everywhere here, steel and otherwise. The ones of which we are most fond are trees that grow to a height of 80 feet, have large, dark green leathery leaves, and from summer into fall produce the most robust flowers (8-10 inches across) you ever laid your eyes on. The association between the South and magnolias is so strong that it's difficult to pronounce magnolia without a drawl.

🐚 **Osprey.** The words "regal" and "majestic" describe this powerful bird of prey. Often mistaken for an eagle, osprey can be distinguished by white feathers dominating underneath with brown feathers topside on wings and back. When they fly their bent-shaped wings span five feet. Osprey fish for a living, swooping down *feet first* and using their gigantic talons to snatch fish literally out of the water. They like to build nests close by tidal water on power poles, bridge-tender roofs, channel markers, and buoys. Osprey mate for life. Human animals sometimes erect tall poles near waterways in hopes of attracting a pair to nest.

🐚 **Sand Dollar.** Though rarely thought of as animals, sand dollars are living, breathing creatures. The five petals you see embossed on their faces are used for filtration and breathing. The center of the flower is a water sucking device providing power for hundreds of tiny tube feet on their undersides. The tube feet move sand dollars around, dig in the sand, and carry food to their mouths. The mouth, at the center of the underside, has tiny teeth for straining and chewing. Factoid: sand dollars stand on end against the current to capture algae floating through the water. Picture rows and rows of them standing on end facing the same direction—a virtual army of sand dollars! Shell seekers must only take sand dollars that are dead (white or brown). If they are still greenish, be sure to return them to deeper water.

 ❦ **Sea Oats.** The tall grass that grows along the dunes of our beaches is a close relative of the grain we grow to eat, but in this case the grain grows wild and provides protection from beach erosion. If you fancy taking some home to display in a vase in your living room, be fore-warned: these plants are so valuable to our beach ecology that it is illegal to cut or pick them, and you could go to jail.

 ❦ **Wading Birds.** Perhaps no animal defines our Sea Islands better than the Great Egret, the statuesque white bird that has become an icon by which many identify the unique landscape of the marsh. Once hunted to the edge of extinction for their prized plumes, egrets now flourish here thanks to past efforts of the Audubon Society. The Great Egret is three to four feet tall, with white plumage, black legs, and a long, yellow bill. When you see a smaller (two-foot) white bird with longer plumes, that's a Snowy Egret. Keep on the lookout for another dazzling bird, the Great Blue Heron. Though four feet tall, this bird is harder to spot because its plumes are blue and grey and blend into the environment. Look for long plumes cascading from its chest area, and long black plumes arching from its eyes toward the back of its head. Stunningly beautiful.

Recommended Reading about Beaufort

OR A MOST COMPLETE ARRAY of books about Beaufort for purchase with knowledgeable and friendly staff to help you, go to **Bay Street Trading Company** located at 808 Bay Street, and to the newly-opened **Firehouse Books** at 706 Craven Street next to the Beaufort County Library. **Beaufort Book Store** in Jean Ribaut Square Shopping Center also has a wide selection and excellent staff. The Greater Beaufort Chamber of Commerce Visitors' Center, 1006 Bay Street, offers a number of books on Beaufort for purchase.

For browsing and to consult out-of-print and rare books, go to the **Beaufort County Library** in the new brick building on Scotts Street and ask for the room that houses books on South Carolina and Beaufort history. These books are not for checkout, so you don't need a library card, but you'll have to stay in the library to read. The librarians are very helpful and can point you in the right direction depending on your particular interests.

Renowned author Pat Conroy grew up on the Point in old Beaufort. Among his novels are *The Water Is Wide*, *The Great Santini* and *The Prince of Tides*. All three have been made into major motion pictures, the latter two being filmed right here in Beaufort. We have become accustomed to seeing movie stars walking around our town, most recently Tom Hanks, Sally Fields, and Kevin Costner during the filming of *Forrest Gump* and *The War* in the summer and fall of 1993.

All of the Conroy novels take place in Beaufort and the nearby Sea Islands. Largely autobiographical, they are full of rapture for the unique beauty of the area. They include fictional characters who bear strong resemblances to local folks, most notably Mr. Fruit from *The Prince of Tides*, who is known locally as "Tutti-Fruitti." If you see a tall, thin, slightly hunched black man with a cap and glasses walking around Beaufort or at Plum's, his favorite hangout, that's he. He is noted for his spontaneous traffic-directing and parade-leading, and is a valued and appreciated member of our community who helps by picking up litter around town, so be sure to bid him good day.

Another renowned author and Beaufort native, Valerie Sayers, has left the indelible mark of her home town on the literary world. Currently the director of creative writing at the University of Notre Dame, Ms. Sayers' works about personal and family relationships have been compared to William Faulkner's novels. She is perhaps best known for *Due East*, her fictional name for Beaufort. Her three other novels also use Beaufort and its surroundings as settings: *Who Do You Love; How I Got Him Back*; and her latest bestseller, *The Distance Between Us*.

In addition to the Conroy and Sayers novels, the following are currently the most popular books about

Beaufort and the surrounding area according to our local booksellers:

❦ *A Guide to Historic Beaufort*, definitive guidebook to historic houses and churches, published by Historic Beaufort Foundation.

❦ *A Sea Island Lady*, by Francis Griswold, saga of the Civil War and Reconstruction in Beaufort, rivals *Gone with the Wind* in scope and intensity.

❦ *Beaufort Cook Book*, by Dee Hryharrow and Isabel M. Hoogenboom, a mouth-watering treasury of Carolina recipes handed down through the generations.

❦ *Ebb Tide - Flood Tide*, photography by local photographer Lynn Mclaren whose credits include National Geographic, a gorgeous pictorial of Beaufort and its Sea Islands.

❦ *Historic Resources of the Lowcountry, A Regional Survey*, prepared by the Lowcountry Council of Governments, is an introduction to the architectural and historic resources of the Lowcountry: Beaufort, Colleton, Hampton and Jasper counties.

❦ *My Friend, The Gullah*, by J. Gary Black, personal conversations and experiences with Gullah-speaking people.

❦ *Plantations of the Lowcountry*, researched by Agnes Baldwin, text by William P. Baldwin, photography by N. Jane Iseley, a beautiful addition to any library.

❦ *Rehearsal for Reconstruction,* by Willie Lee Rose, superb history of the Sea Islands during Federal occupation, winner of three prestigious prizes for historical writing including the Francis Parkman Award.

❦ *Reminiscences of Sea Island Heritage,* by Ron Daise, documents the lifestyles, customs, superstitions and folklore of St. Helena Island.

❦ *Sands of Time,* by Margaret Greer, attractive pictorial book giving overview of Beaufort history.

❦ *Sea Island Seasons,* a delightful collection of favorite recipes contributed by residents of Beaufort, published by Beaufort County Open Land Trust.

❦ *South Carolina's Lowcountry, A Past Preserved,* text by Catherine Campani Messmer, photography by C. Andrew Halcomb, a pictorial study of three historic towns: Beaufort, Charleston and Georgetown.

❦ *Tales of Beaufort,* by Nell Graydon, stories about the houses, town and county of Beaufort. Also *South Carolina Ghost Tales* by same author, wonderful to read to children.

❦ *Tideland Treasures,* by Todd Ballantine, a naturalist's guide to beaches and salt marshes of the Lowcountry. Grab this and go to the beach.

❦ *Touring the South Carolina Backroads,* by Nancy Rhyne, includes a tour of historic downtown Beaufort and an extraordinary treat, a "witch-doctor tour" from

Sheldon ruins to Hunting Island State Park.

❦ *When Roots Die,* by Patricia Jones-Jackson, comprehensive study of the language of Gullah, an endangered speech on the Sea Islands.

Be sure also to savor a special literary genre whose roots run deep in Beaufort history: Civil War diaries. The young Northern soldiers, missionaries, and entrepreneurs who lived in Beaufort and on the surrounding islands during the Civil War included some extraordinarily literate and sensitive people, both men and women. Their diaries constitute a treasure trove of information about wartime conditions here, the human drama of the Federal occupation, and the thrill of the emancipation of the slaves. We especially commend, and give thanks for the use of excerpts in this book from, the following diaries, most of which are currently available in excellent paperback editions: *The Journal of Charlotte L. Forten,* edited by Ray Allen Billington; *A Woman's Civil War, Esther Hill Hawks' Diary,* edited by Gerald Schwartz; *Army Life in a Black Regiment,* which is the diary of Thomas Wentworth Higginson; and *Letters and Diary of Laura M. Towne,* edited by Rupert Sargent Holland. ❧

Major Motion Pictures About Beaufort

WHEN *The Great Santini* was filmed here in 1977-78, no one could foresee the impact it would have on Beaufort. Not only did the movie make Beaufort known to the millions of people who saw it, it also revealed our town as a perfect location to portray many different moments in time. The carefully preserved old houses in the historic district look as they did when originally built, spanning almost three centuries. The downtown business district looks as it did in the 1940's and 1950's. And the massive live oak trees and verdant salt marshes portray the majesty and beauty of eternal nature. For these reasons, and because Beaufort has enjoyed such a rich cultural history, the film industry has continued to take great interest in Beaufort, both as a location and as a subject matter.

Box Office Hits

❦ *The Great Santini*: This was a major box office hit in the late 1970's, an especially fitting beginning for film making in Beaufort because Pat Conroy, the author of the book, grew up on the Point in Beaufort's historic district. Mr. Conroy wrote this novel about his real-life father, a rugged U.S. Marine Corps jet pilot stationed at the Marine Corps Air Station at Beaufort, with whom Pat had a struggling personal relationship. Robert Duvall starred as the father, earning himself an Academy Award nomination for Best Actor. Blythe Danner played the mother. The historic home on the Point known as Tidalholm was the location for this film.

🐝 *Conrack*: This film was adapted from another fine novel by local author Pat Conroy entitled *The Water Is Wide*. While the movie was actually filmed on the coast in nearby Georgia, it is about Mr. Conroy's experiences and struggles as a school teacher educating the children of an isolated black community on Daufuskie Island in Beaufort County. Jon Voight portrayed Pat Conroy in the leading role in this film.

🐝 *The Big Chill*: One of the most popular films of the 1980's, this is the story of college friends who reunite after many years when one of their classmates dies. With its terrific Motown soundtrack and all-star cast including William Hurt, Jeff Goldblum, Glenn Close, Meg Tilly, Jobeth Williams, Mary Kay Place, Kevin Kline and Tom Berenger, this film is an enduring hit. It includes beautiful scenes of Bay Street, Beaufort River, the Chapel of Ease and, especially, Tidalholm on the Point. The entire movie is centered around this historic old house, which also served as the location for *The Great Santini*. Folks have now gotten into the habit of calling Tidalholm "The Big Chill House."

Beaufort, 1864

We had a new camp on Port Royal Island, very pleas-
antly situated, just out of Beaufort. It stretched nearly to
the edge of a shelving bluff, fringed with pines and overlooking the river; below the bluff was a hard, narrow beach,
where one might gallop a mile and bathe at the farther
end . . . . The new camp was named Camp Shaw, in honor
of the noble young officer who had lately fallen at Fort
Wagner, under circumstances which had endeared him to
all the men.

—Col. Thomas Wentworth Higginson

❦ *Glory*: This extraordinary film about the Massachusetts 54th Regiment, America's first unit of black soldiers during the Civil War, won Oscars for Cinematog-
raphy, Sound, and Best Supporting Actor (Denzel Washington). The 54th Regiment, under the command of
Colonel Robert Shaw, was quartered in Beaufort during
the Civil War and left here on its bloody rendezvous with
destiny at Fort Wagner near Charleston. Parts of the film
were shot in rural areas surrounding Beaufort, which have
remained much the same as they looked during the Civil
War. The Public Broadcasting System subsequently filmed
a documentary production here on the same subject, aired
under the title *The Massachusetts 54th*.

❦ *The Prince of Tides*: Nominated for a number of significant Academy Awards including Best Actor and Best
Picture, this film was made in Beaufort in the spring and

summer of 1990. The stars, Barbra Streisand (who also directed) and Nick Nolte, resided on the Point during the months of filming. Again, this is based on a semi-autobiographical novel by Pat Conroy about a Beaufort family's struggle in coming to terms with its past. The large white house portrayed in the film as the one Tom Wingo grew up in is really Bay Street Inn. The house Pat Conroy actually grew up in is several blocks away.

🦌 *Daughters of the Dust*: This underground classic, subsequently released in selected theaters across the nation, has caused a sensation among followers of non-Hollywood film making. It is about the matriarchal nature of Gullah society.

NEW RELEASES

🦌 *Forrest Gump*: Due to be released in the summer of 1994, this film follows the life of a boy who is raised on the coast of South Carolina and becomes a shrimper. Filming was done in many places in and around Beaufort, including Fripp Island where Tom Hanks stayed with his family. Sally Fields co-stars with Hanks in what is expected to be a big hit.

🦌 *The War*: This film is about a poor Southern family that becomes entangled in a "war" over a tree home. Portions of the movie were filmed by the tree at Grady's Point. Kevin Costner is one of the adult stars in this movie for children, due to be released in 1994.

HITS MADE FOR TELEVISION

❦ *Charlotte Forten's Mission*: American Playhouse produced this film for the Public Broadcasting System, the true story of Charlotte Forten, a wealthy black Philadelphia missionary who traveled to St. Helena Island in 1862 to help educate the newly freed black slaves. Her diary has become one of the major historical resources about the role of women during the Civil War. Some noteworthy Beaufortonians had speaking parts in the film. We think they did at least as well as many of the professionals. There are gorgeous scenes of the islands and waterways surrounding Beaufort.

St. Helena Island, January 1, 1863 [Emancipation Day]

The most glorious day this nation has yet seen, *I* think . I thought I had never seen a sight so beautiful. There were the black soldiers, in their blue coats and scarlett pants, the officers of this and other regiments in their handsome uniforms, and crowds of lookers-on, men, women and children, grouped in various attitudes, under the trees. The faces all wore a happy, eager, expectant look.

—Charlotte Forten

❦ *Family Across the Sea*: Sponsored by the South Carolina Humanities Council and aired on the Public Broadcasting System, this emotionally moving documentary follows a delegation of Gullah people currently living on the Sea Islands surrounding Beaufort as they visit the nation of Sierra Leone in Africa. A direct cultural link exists between the Gullah community here and the present-day residents of Sierra Leone, some of whose ancestors were brought here during the days of slavery. This excellent documentary explores these links and celebrates the reunion of these people. Emory Campbell, Director of Penn Center on St. Helena Island, was a member of the delegation that traveled to Sierra Leone and was made an honorary chief of that nation. 🌿

Cultural Events and Entertainment

EVEN though we enjoy a small-town atmosphere here in Beaufort, our community has always attracted superb artists and has developed numerous cultural events and organizations. You can pick up a calendar of special events at the Greater Beaufort Chamber of Commerce Visitors' Center. Current events are listed in the local daily newspaper, *The Beaufort Gazette*, or you can call the organizations listed below for more information.

ORGANIZATIONS

🦌 **Arts Council of Northern Beaufort County, 521-4144,** provides technical assistance, information, and referral on local cultural events. "A Taste of the Arts" series of parties and entertaining is a popular fund-raiser. Call to find out what's going on culturally in the area.

🦌 **Beaufort Art Association, 521-4144,** promotes community interest and education in the visual arts. Its annual Spring Art Show in March features the best works of local artists.

🦌 **Beaufort Chamber Orchestra Guild, 521-4144,** puts on concerts at the USCB Performing Arts Center and around town.

❦ **Beaufort County Open Land Trust, 521-2175,** preserves vistas and open spaces, raising funds by sponsoring special events such as coaching day (antique horse-driven coaches on parade), gala raffles, special luncheons, and dinner plantation tours.

❦ **Beaufort Film Society, 521-4144,** a new group, presents a variety of foreign and classic films; holds lectures and seminars on films and the film industry by invited guest speakers; and serves as a clearing house on film opportunities in the Lowcountry.

❦ **Beaufort Little Theatre, 525-4144,** puts on plays at the Performing Arts Center at USCB on Carteret Street. Tickets can be purchased at the door in most cases.

❦ **Byrne Miller Dance Theatre, 524-9148,** sponsors top-ranking dance troupes from all over the world performing at Lasseter Theatre at the Marine Corps Air Station or at the USCB Performing Arts Center on Carteret Street. Tickets are usually available at the door.

❦ **Creative Retirement Center, 521-4113,** is a seniors' program sponsored by USCB, affiliated with Elderhostel Institute Network. It offers classes, lectures and travel. Its members do volunteer work in the community.

❦ **Greater Beaufort Jazz Association, 521-4144,** is dedicated to the promotion, performance and education of jazz. It sponsors an ongoing event called Second Sunday Jazz Series, featuring jazz concerts at varying locations every second Sunday of the month.

Historic Beaufort Foundation, 524-6334, encourages historic preservation in Beaufort. This foundation sponsors the well-known annual Fall Tour of Homes. Each May 14 the Lafayette Soiree, an auction and dinner-dance, is held to benefit the foundation. It operates its headquarters building, the John Mark Verdier House, 801 Bay Street, as a house museum, open to the public.

🦌 **Main Street Beaufort USA, 525-6644,** is dedicated to historic preservation and revitalization downtown. It sponsors promotional events such as Night on the Town, Downtown Diversions, Beaufort by the Bay Winefest, Farmers Market, and more.

🦌 **University of South Carolina at Beaufort (USCB), 521-4100,** sponsors numerous cultural events in its Performing Arts Center on Carteret Street. A cultural series is offered from September through April (call 521-4144 for information on this series). In addition to a full curriculum of normal academic subjects, the University offers classes in all kinds of arts.

ANNUAL FESTIVALS AND SPECIAL EVENTS

Beaufort is blessed with an extraordinarily favorable climate, far enough south for relatively mild weather all year round and far enough north to enjoy four distinct seasons. This makes for festivals and special events throughout the year. Here are the most significant ones:

❦ **January.** The South Carolina Humanities Council has designated Beaufort as the site of its Humanities Festival, featuring events focused on the unique cultural characteristics of our Sea Islands. Cosponsored by the Arts Council of Northern Beaufort County, the Beaufort Humanities Festival is a continuing, annual event to kick off the "Beaufort Season," the year-round series of community and cultural events described below. The Humanities Festival arrives in January at a time when Beaufort is vibrant and beautiful while most of the rest of the country is in the doldrums of winter.

❦ **February.** Spring gets an early start in this neck of the woods with the Daffodil Festival, weeks of blooming daffodils in mid-February. That's a wonderful time to visit, as the climate warms up and one can enjoy an early springtime here. For a particularly stunning sight, drive to Cane Island to see the daffodil fields; a virtual carpet of yellow awaits you. For a nominal fee, you can pick your own. When flowers are blooming, there will be signs along Highway 802 on Lady's Island pointing to Cane Island near the McTeer Bridge.

❦ **March.** The St. Helena's Spring Tour of Homes is usually held the third weekend in March and features tours of privately-owned historic homes and plantations in the Beaufort area. The tours attract visitors from all over the world, so make reservations for accommodations early. For more information and a free brochure, call its sponsor, St. Helena's Episcopal Church, 522-1712.

❦ **March-April.** The Azalea Bloom, beginning in mid-March and continuing through mid-April, is a major reason for the stunning beauty of the Lowcountry in springtime. The large blooms appear in masses in gardens everywhere, white, pink and lavender. During this special time the Council of Beaufort Garden Clubs sponsors flower shows. Call the Chamber of Commerce, 524-3163, for information.

❦ **May.** The Gullah Festival is a celebration of Sea Island heritage that attracts visitors from all over the world. It showcases gospel, jazz, storytelling, Gullah language translation, fine-arts displays, folklore, and arts and crafts. This festival has gained recognition as one of the most important celebrations of African-American culture in the nation. The festival is held on Memorial Day weekend with activities centered around the downtown waterfront park. For more information call 521-4144.

❦ **June-July.** In midsummer the Farmers Market takes place every Saturday from 8 a.m. 'til noon, offering the best fresh local produce for sale. Arts and crafts by local artisans are also available. Call Main Street Beaufort USA for more information at 525-6644.

❦ **July.** Perhaps Beaufort's biggest event of the year, the Beaufort Water Festival celebrates our reverence for that which so blessedly surrounds us—the sea. Lasting almost two weeks, the Water Festival has its roots in the antebellum tradition of plantation owners' racing barges on these waters. Among the featured events are boat races, fishing tournaments, the famed bed race, aerial shows, dances, concerts, a hometown parade, antique and art and craft shows, a beauty pageant, water ski shows and more. Reservations for accommodations should be made far in advance, especially if you wish to stay in the downtown area. Bring your boat if you have one; the sandbar in the Beaufort River gets very populated for this event. For a brochure and more information call 524-0600.

🦌 **October.** The Historic Beaufort Foundation Fall Tour of Homes usually takes place the second week in October and features tours of privately-owned historic homes and plantations in the area. The Fall Tour of Homes attracts visitors from all over the world, so make your arrangements for accommodations in advance. For a brochure and information call its sponsor, Historic Beaufort Foundation at 524-6334.

Beaufort by the Bay Winefest takes place in the farmers market area of the downtown waterfront park and features wines for tasting. Both domestic and international fine wines are offered as well as fine food from the best local restaurants and great local musical entertainment. Call Main Street Beaufort USA at 525-6644 .

🦌 **November.** The Beaufort County Open Land Trust has a Fall Tour of Homes, or a fund-raising event, the first weekend in November.

On the second Saturday in November comes the St. Helena Episcopal Church Annual Bazaar. Bargain hunters and crafts lovers alike will love this church bazaar held from 10 a.m. to 3 p.m. Handmade items, plants, used books and clothes and plenty of tasty food can be purchased from the friendly parishioners.

Also in November is Heritage Days. This event is a benefit/celebration of African-American and Sea Island culture for Penn Center. Held on the beautiful Penn Center campus on St. Helena Island, Heritage Days takes place over three days (the second weekend in November) and features African-American art exhibitions, a symposium, a fish fry, blues singing, a parade, folk arts and Lowcountry foods. Call 838-2432 for more information.

🦌 **December.** The Christmas Season is special in Beaufort. With downtown all decorated, it recaptures the spirit of Christmases in years past. Parking meters are holiday wrapped for the month of December; free parking is a gift from the city and Main Street Beaufort USA. Window-decoration contests, tree-lighting ceremonies, a parade of festooned boats in the bay at dusk, and a real old-fashioned Christmas parade down Bay Street are just a few of the events that enhance the holiday season.

A particularly enjoyable December event is Night On The Town. For one night in early December the merchants in downtown Beaufort open their doors to invite customers in for homemade goodies and Christmas cheer as a way of thanking them for their patronage. The street is closed so that people can meander freely. Entertainment ranging from jazz to madrigals is on every corner.

The evening climate at this time of year is especially pleasant and lends itself to walking out of doors. For information, contact Main Street Beaufort USA at 525-6644.

NIGHTTIME ENTERTAINMENT

🍌 **Bananas, 910 Bay Street, 522-0910,** features topnotch local jazz entertainment on Wednesday and Saturday nights.

🍌 **The Bank Waterfront Grill and Bar, 926 Bay Street, 522-8831,** offers a variety of musical entertainment on weekends.

🍌 **Blackstone's, 915 Bay Street, 524-4330,** presents one-act productions throughout the year. Beaufort's budding thespians have made this the place for good local theatre. Folk and country music is occasionally performed by talented local artists.

🍌 **The Gadsby Tavern, 822 Bay Street, 525-1800,** occasionally features solo performers (guitarists/singers, etc.) on the weekends. Outdoor seating is available with a view of the water.

🍌 **The Gullah House, 838-2402,** on Highway 21 on St. Helena Island has excellent jazz ensembles on Fridays, Saturdays, and special occasions.

🍌 **Ping's Sports Bar & Grill, 917 Bay Street, 521-2545.** Sports fans will want to watch all the big games at Ping's. This establishment also offers musical entertainment for the less athletically inclined. Beef and seafood specialties are served for lunch and dinner.

❦ **Plaza 8 Theaters, Beaufort Plaza, 524-9468,** gets all the best movies, even those that aren't filmed in Beaufort. Discounted tickets can be bought for weekend matinees and Tuesday nights. Grab a bucket of popcorn from the concession stand and enjoy the show. Call for current features and show times.

❦ **Plums at Night, 904 ½ Bay Street, 525-1946,** has rhythm and blues bands on Friday and Saturday nights when dancing becomes infectious. For more daring individuals, there is an open mike on Thursday nights. Open Thursday through Sunday nights. Hot and cold sandwiches and reasonably priced drinks. ❧

Guide to Shopping in Beaufort

WHILE suburban America has made enclosed malls as plentiful as interstate connectors, downtown Beaufort keeps trucking along with superb traditional shopping. For starters, we present to you downtown Beaufort's answer to anchor tenants, stores that have bonded our downtown together for generations:

DOWNTOWN GENERAL MERCHANDISE STORES

🦌 **Fordham Hardware, 701 Bay Street, 524-3161,** is the kind of hardware store you remember from your childhood, everything imaginable a hardware merchant should carry from nails by the ounce to fertilizer and wheelbarrows. If you need it, Fordham's has it.

🦌 **Lipsitz Department Store, 825 Bay Street, 524-2330,** is famous for shoes, selling Stride Rite, Top Sider, Keds, Rockport, Mother Goose and Naturalizers since long before you and I remember. They are also headquarters for Oshkosh, Levi and other good old American brands. And their prices are good old American bargains.

DOWNTOWN SPECIALTY SHOPS

Downtown Beaufort has become a haven of specialty retail shops. The stores listed below are just some of the places to shop downtown. Find what fits your tastes.

🦌 **Bay Street Jewelers, 902 Bay Street, 524-4165,** displays a wide selection of jewelry, timepieces, wedding accessories and gifts for everyone.

🦌 **Bay Street Trading Company, 808 Bay Street, 524-2000,** has an excellent collection of books, especially on the Sea Islands and the Lowcountry. Also offers fine stationery and nautical charts.

🦌 **Beaufort Emporium, 723 Bay Street, 524-3726,** features cookware, candles, hobbyist model kits, patio decorations, and everything you need for picnics and parties.

🦌 **Beaufort Office Supply, 720 Bay Street, 524-3726.** The friendly owners of this store will help you find any sundry items that you may have forgotten to pack and a calendar to write down all of the special events in Beaufort, in addition to normal office supplies.

🦌 **Blackstone's, 915 Bay Street, 524-4330,** offers groceries and gourmet items, also a cafe and deli serving coffee and sandwiches. Beer and wine also available.

🦌 **Boombears, 501 Carteret Street, 524-2525,** offers a wide variety of toys, stuffed animals, games, and gifts for children and adults. A world famous shop.

🦌 **Buttons & Bows, 813 Bay Street, 525-6373,** specializes in wedding and party clothes, everything for the blushing bride. It has a wide selection of formal and semi-formal gowns and dresses, as well as a complete catalog selection if you don't see that perfect dress in the shop. Shoes and accessories complete the ensemble.

❦ **The Chocolate Tree, 507 Carteret, 524-7980,** makes chocolate, shipped all over the world. You can watch candy-making in action here. Forget the calories and indulge. A chocoholic's paradise.

❦ **The Craftseller, 818 Bay Street, 525-6104,** has lots of hand-crafted pottery and stoneware, hand-crafted jewelry, wind chimes, candles, and other items.

❦ **Deal's, 724 Bay Street, 524-4993,** is a men's and women's clothing store specializing in Irish imported apparel. Fine wool sweaters, durable denim jumpers and sturdy cotton shirts of all kinds. The emphasis is on classic cuts, natural fibers, durability and discounts.

❦ **Finders Keepers, 920 Bay Street, 525-9200,** offers an array of items from postcards to costume jewelry to knickknacks. And, if you don't feel like going to Hunting Island to look for seashells on the beach, you'll find all of the seashells your heart desires here.

❦ **The Garden Party, 102 West Street, 522-8634,** on the waterfront where West Street has been extended as a wide walkway, in the new building that looks old timey. Features garden items, house plants and gifts. Great rocking chairs on the porch, so come sit and people-watch.

❦ **Glad Rags and Flags, 810 King Street, 525-9095,** near the post office, has a vivid assortment of colorful flags and wind socks to decorate breezy porches.

🦌 **Jasmine, 919 Bay Street, 524-6660,** in Old Bay Marketplace, features fashionable women's apparel and accessories. Shop here for your casual resort wear.

🦌 **La Residence, 901 Port Republic Street 522-8805,** features fine linens and accessories for bed and bath. Among the items in this store are linens by Jane Wilner, Matouk, Peacock Alley and Imperial, and scented bath oils, picture frames and gifts.

🦌 **Lowcountry Bicycles, 904 Port Republic Street, 524-9585,** has everything for bicycle enthusiast and beginner. Top quality bicycles in all configurations are available here, as well as accessories and clothing. Get your roller-blades here, too. Excellent repairs and service. Bicycles for rent too, a good way to see the sights.

🦌 **Old Bay Marketplace, 917 Bay Street,** is a small, old-timey downtown covered mall with boutique shops including women's apparel, ice-cream parlor, jewelry store, beauty parlor and shoe shine stand. You may enter both from Bay and Port Republic Streets.

🦌 **Plumage, 104 West Street, 522-8807,** offers women's apparel, from resort wear to elegant evening dresses, in a handsome new building on the waterfront that looks like it has been here for a century.

🦌 **Precious Cargo, 904 Bay Street, 525-1075,** has elegant gifts galore, from glassware to oriental vases, serving trays and more. Imaginative and colorful window displays entice you to come in and browse.

❦ **Sashay, 1100 Carteret Street, 524-7667.** At the end of Carteret Street across from USCB you will find this pretty clothing store. Women's fashions from casual to cocktail dresses can be purchased here.

❦ **Sea Island Lady Too, 210 Scott Street, 522-8910,** offers dresses, separates and lingerie with an eye toward youthful, casual style. And for the wildest earrings and jewelry in town, you need look no farther.

❦ **Sea Island Mercantile & Provisioning, Inc., 928 Bay Street, 522-3000,** offers a collection of delicious Lowcountry seafood and confections, including famous she-crab soup, oyster stew, Vidalia onion salad dressing, sweet spring green tomato relish, and more. Pick up one of their catalog brochures. You can order delicacies for mail delivery to your home or gift baskets to friends.

❦ **The Shop, 608 North Street 524-7383,** near Carteret Street, specializes in T-shirts. Great selection. Their "live wild shrimp" aquariums featuring live local fish and shellfish in natural habitats are not to be missed.

ANTIQUES

❦ **Bellavista Antiques and Interiors, 206 Carteret Street, 521-0687,** is a large shop filled with antiques and unusual decorative items. A fun place to browse.

❦ **Chitty & Company Antiques, 812 Port Republic Street, 524-7889,** have European and Oriental collectibles, antique furniture, lamps, shades, silver and china. For fine antiques, this is the place. You will enjoy talking to the cultivated and gregarious owners, Penny and Charles Chitty.

❦ **The Collectors' Antique Mall and Craft Shops, 208 Carteret Street, 522-8228,** features all kinds of accessories and antiques. Large selection.

❦ **The Consignor's Antique Mall, 913 Port Republic Street, 521-0660,** is filled with a wide variety of antiques and crafts. You can find furniture, toys and glassware as well as brightly painted chairs. In back is a tea room with light fare to keep you happy while you shop.

❦ **Den of Antiquity, Highway 170, 521-9990,** across the Broad and Chechessee Rivers in the direction of Savannah and Hilton Head Island, about a twenty-minute drive from downtown. This store has old furniture, glass, china, books, and old farm implements.

❦ **MacPherson's Antiques, 1106 Carteret Street, 524-4678,** offers American country antiques as well as unusual gadgets, china, glassware, and antique clothing.

❦ **Michael Rainey's Antiques, 702 Craven Street, 521-4532.** An elegant shop, Michael Rainey's specializes in eighteenth and early nineteenth century American furniture and accessories. Antiques include beds, desks, china, chairs, fireplace accessories, and miniature chests.

❦ **Port Royal Antiques, 913 Bay Street, 524-6357,** offers a variety of collectibles including china, glassware, crystal, hand-crafted gifts and collectibles. Great T-shirts.

🦌 **Southern Antiques, 807 Bay Street, 524-8554,** has used furniture and authentic antiques, most with American country flavor. Everything is here from old stoves to oak dressers, rocking chairs, accent pieces and collectibles.

🦌 **Thorndike Williams Interior Design, 308 Scott Street, 524-7688,** offers exquisite European and Oriental collectibles, a variety of gift items, decorative fabrics and beautiful antiques.

ARTWORK & GALLERIES

Original artwork from Lowcountry artists and others is available at a number of galleries. Take some of the culture of our Sea Islands home with you.

🦌 **Art Images, 103 Charles Street, 524-2877,** behind "Its Me Too!" near the waterfront park, has a wide selection of watercolor art featuring Lowcountry scenes and flowers, both realistic and impressionistic.

🦌 **W. Jackson Causey Studio, 805 Craven Street, 524-2595.** Will Causey, known nationwide for his realistic American scenes, aptly describes himself as a "painter of God's creation and its beauty, a chronicler of human achievements and our heritage." Be sure to visit his studio to view his mixed media artwork.

🦌 **The Checkered Moon, 208 West Street, 522-3466,** has whimsical artwork, beautiful hand-quilted clothing, handmade semiprecious stone jewelry and more. This shop explodes with color and is fun to explore.

🦌 **Frogmore Frolics, Highway 21 south, 838-9102,** at Frogmore on St. Helena Island, has everything from watercolors to sculpture to clothing crafts and accessories. Look for the sign with the frog on it.

🦌 **Gallery One, 824 Bay Street, 524-7967,** near the main entrance to the waterfront park, has a large selection of watercolor art with emphasis on the Lowcountry.

🦌 **Indigo Gallery, 809 Bay Street, 524-1036,** offers reasonably-priced prints of Carolina fish, fowl, flora and fauna. The talented owners will also frame your pictures.

🦌 **Suzanne and Eric Longo Gallery, 407 Carteret Street, 522-8933.** The Longo's creations are contemporary art works, both paintings and sculptures for indoors and out. Suzanne does ceramic sculptures, and Eric creates vibrant paintings.

🦌 **Red Piano Too Gallery, Highway 21 south, 838-2241,** at Frogmore on St. Helena Island, has a superb selection by local artists, with a penchant for folk art. Jewelry and sculpture, as well as furniture, complete the contents of this large, airy gallery.

🦌 **Rhett Gallery, 901 Bay Street, 524-3339,** features original prints and paintings of the Lowcountry by renowned artist Nancy Ricker Rhett, as well as Audubon prints, antique nautical charts, botanicals, natural history prints, Civil War art, and custom framing. 🦌

Guide to Dining in Beaufort

W HATEVER YOUR TASTE, you'll find a place to please your palate in Beaufort. Numerous downtown restaurants are interspersed among the shops along Bay Street, and there are more on the roads leading to town, some especially nice ones on Lady's Island.

FINE DINING

🍃 **The Anchorage, 1103 Bay Street, 524-9392,** offers a continental menu including seafood, steaks, and pasta dishes. Dine in Old World elegance overlooking the Bay in a mansion that dates back to 1770. The atmosphere is quiet and formal. Also open for lunch. Reservations recommended.

🍃 Try **Emily's, 906 Port Republic Street, 522-1866,** for a special feast. If you are in the mood for lighter fare, sample the various tapas ("little meals" in Spanish) similar to appetizers, which are ever-changing and abundant. The menu is fresh and varied, the food excellent, the ambiance sophisticated, elegant and intimate. Prices are moderate to expensive.

🍃 **Rhett House Inn, 1009 Craven Street, 524-9030,** operates as a four-star bed & breakfast, providing a gourmet restaurant on premises to serve guests and the general public on a reservation-only basis. The imaginative, outstanding menu is prix fixe at $35.00 per person and changes frequently. Open Wednesday through Saturday for one seating at 7:30 p.m.

🦌 **Wilkop's Whitehall Inn, U.S. 21, 521-1915,** just across the downtown bridge on Lady's Island. Look for the big white house with porches on your right. Offers consistently fine continental cuisine with an eye toward keeping happy the very loyal local clientele. Also open for lunch. Prices are moderate to expensive. Reservations recommended.

🦌 **Whitehall Plantation Inn, Lady's Island, 521-1700,** a hard right-hand turn immediately across the downtown bridge. The best sunset view in town, overlooking the water and marsh. The menu is straightforward and crowd-pleasing, everything is prepared to perfection, and the service is excellent. Open for lunch too.

The Islands: Tropical, Greek and Local

🦌 In the mood for a tropical island atmosphere? Then **Bananas, 910 Bay Street, 522-0910,** is your kind of place. Great frozen tropical drinks, appetizers, burgers, ribs and salads, and always lots of fun. Great jazz entertainment is featured as well. Open Sundays and lunch time too.

🦌 For Greek cuisine try **John Cross Tavern, upstairs at 812 Bay Street, 524-3993.** A longtime hangout, this tavern has hosted actor Tom Berenger and newsman Walter Cronkite, among other celebrities. Some swear they have seen the ghost of John Cross from time to time in this old building which hasn't changed much since colonial days. Authentic Greek cuisine, seafood and steaks in a casual atmosphere.

🦌 When you want down home local cookin', try **The Gullah House, 838-2402,** on St. Helena Island at Frogmore. Local homemade favorites like crab cakes, "swimps" (shrimp), bean stew, gumbo, Lowcountry boil, country fried steak, and salads and sandwiches with down home flavor are among the offerings. Don't leave without trying the sweet potato chips; they're out of this world. Open for lunch and dinner. Closed Mondays.

SEAFOOD/STEAKS/ETC.

🦌 **The Bank, 926 Bay Street, 522-8831.** As its name implies, this used to be one of Beaufort's commercial banks. You can feast on seafood and steaks or have a drink in the upstairs bar. The menu also offers sandwiches and lighter fare. The Bank overlooks beautiful Beaufort Bay and is open for lunch and dinner.

🦌 **The Gadsby Tavern, 822 Bay Street, 522-1800,** has recently undergone a change in ownership with a new look and a changed menu. Everything from seafood to steaks is offered here, and the food is consistently good. The atmosphere is intimate and elegant in the front, becoming more casual toward the back where the bar faces the waterfront park. Outdoor dining is available overlooking the water, and entertainment is provided on weekends.

❦ **Plum's, 904 ½ Bay Street, 525-1946.** A favorite nighttime hangout for the locals, Plums serves delicious pasta, seafood and chicken dishes as well as salads and sandwiches. The ice cream here is homemade (really) and wonderful, so save plenty of room for dessert. After your meal, sit on the porch and have a drink as you listen to Beaufort's best blues and look at the waterfront.

❦ **The Steamer, Lady's Island, 522-0210,** has excellent local seafood and delicious beef. This restaurant is always crowded but doesn't take reservations. You'll probably wait awhile for your dinner, but it's all worth it. Fresh shrimp, oysters, clams, crab and lobster are among the offerings, also local fish from flounder to grouper to shark. A local favorite is Frogmore stew, piled high with shrimp, potatoes, onions and sausage in spices. Take Highway 21 over the Lady's Island bridge just past the intersection with 802. It's on your right in a gray wood building with a dirt parking lot.

PIZZA/ITALIAN

❦ **Cinelli's, Highway 280, 525-0910,** prides itself on homemade pizza with strictly fresh toppings. Run by an Italian family, it offers some pasta dishes and salads as well. Dining is casual and reasonably priced. Located a little bit of a drive from downtown in the Shell Point Shopping Plaza past the Parris Island main gate.

🦌 **The Upper Crust, Lady's Island, 521-1999,** has fresh pizza with toppings of crab, lobster and shrimp, also subs and sandwiches. Try the white pizza, made with olive oil base, herbs and spices.

LUNCH

Lunch is a favorite time of day in Beaufort, and the restaurants make it especially enjoyable. If you stay in town more than a day or two, you will be sure to see familiar faces wherever you dine. Many of the breakfast and dinner restaurants also serve lunch, so be sure to refer to their listings too. Some restaurants serve nothing but lunch. Here are local lunchtime favorites:

🦌 **Bay Towne Grille, 310 West Street, 522-3880,** serves pizza by the slice, sandwiches and salads. Specialties are the Greek sub, the hot pepper cheese and tomato sandwich, and the black bean enchilada. They have counter service, takeout service, and umbrella tables.

🦌 **Blackstone's, 915 Bay Street, 524-4330,** offers the best roast beef sandwich in town. They have a full deli here, so you can have made-to-order sandwiches. Grab a newspaper and have a seat at one of the tables or go across the street to picnic in the waterfront park.

Plums, 904 ½ Bay Street, 525-1946, is an airy cafe with seating available inside and out, overlooking the waterfront park. They serve delicious sandwiches and homemade soups and salads. Try the Florentine delight, an open-faced turkey sandwich on pumpernickel with hollandaise on top—delicious. They also make their own ice cream. Barbra Streisand, while filming *The Prince of Tides*, had her own flavor made to order, named after the movie title. Try a scoop.

Shrimp Shack, St. Helena Island, 838-2962, on the way to Hunting Island State Park, serves delicious local seafood in unusual ways including shrimp burgers and clam strips. Strictly roadside, but no one who drives out to Fripp or Hunting Island can resist stopping for a bite. During the winter call before you make a special trip because they have seasonal hours.

Sgt. White's Diner, 1908 Boundary Street, 522-2029, is a takeout place with down-home offerings. Fried chicken, barbecue and pecan pie are just a few of the possibilities. This place is famous locally for authentic southern cookin'.

Sweet Temptations, 205 West Street, 524-6171, serves sandwiches with fresh baked goodies for dessert, including the best brownies and cinnamon twists in the world.

BREAKFAST

It used to be that finding a breakfast place in the little town of Beaufort was difficult, but not any longer. Here are our favorite breakfast spots:

🦌 **Bay Cafe and Ice Creams, Old Bay Marketplace, 525-6115,** serves delicious doughnuts and pastries along with your favorite eggs, bacon and coffee. Sandwiches are also served at lunchtime. Open at 7:00 a.m.

🦌 **Blackstone's, 915 Bay Street, 524-4330,** is open daily at 8:00 a.m. Have a light breakfast of fresh fruit and home-made muffins or croissants, or try their eggs cooked to order with a side order of grits.

🦌 **Denny's, 1811 Ribaut Road, 524-1151,** is a good choice for a full breakfast if you're on your way out to Parris Island. Located at 1811 Ribaut Road, about three miles from downtown, open 24 hours.

🦌 **Firehouse Books, 706 Craven Street, 522-2665,** combines a superb book store and an espresso bar into a delightful place for coffee and muffins in the morning and all day long. Open every day except Mondays.

🦌 **The Gullah House, 838-2402,** on Highway 21 on St. Helena Island, has hearty local-style breakfasts like fish n' grits and salmon cakes, hash n' eggs, as well as the great standards like buttermilk pancakes, french toast, biscuits and omelets. Breakfast is served Friday through Sunday.

❦ **Harry's, 812 Bay Street, 524-3993,** below John Cross Tavern, is open early for breakfast Monday through Saturday and later on Sundays, serving bacon and egg full breakfasts.

❦ **Shoney's, 524-9571,** is located on Highway 21 north toward the Marine Corps Air Station in the Beaufort Plaza Shopping Center and offers your standard full breakfast fare. Open at 6:00 a.m. every day.

❦ **Sweet Temptations, 205 West Street, 524-6171.** This bakery offers freshly baked breads, muffins and rolls 8:00 a.m. to 4:00 p.m. Monday through Saturday. The aroma of freshly baked cinnamon rolls entices you to start your day here. ❧

Other Good Things to Know About Downtown Beaufort

WHEN YOU KNOW where to go to get those special things that make life a treat, your day can be particularly pleasant. If you're a visitor or a newcomer to Beaufort, you'll be especially pleased to know about the following:

MISCELLANY

🦌 **Where to Buy Sundries Downtown:** If you're looking for film, beer, wine, ice, cigarettes, soda, cookies, candy, ice cream, deodorant, and a limited selection of medicines for colds, go to Blackstone's at 915 Bay Street, or the Beaufort Marina Store located at the downtown marina, which also has tide charts.

🦌 **The Closest Supermarkets to Downtown:** Piggly Wiggly at intersection of Ribaut Road and Highway 21. The Bi-Lo in Jean Ribaut Plaza on Highway 21 has been recently remodeled, with a delightful deli and bakery. The Winn Dixie, just a little way across the river on Lady's Island, also has a deli and bakery.

🦌 **The Closest Drug Stores to Downtown:** Go to Prescriptions Only on Carteret Street across from Budget Print Center. For a full-service drug store, it's Eckerds next to the Winn Dixie supermarket on Lady's Island.

🍄 **The Closest Department Stores to Downtown**: Belk Simpson and K-Mart at Jean Ribaut Plaza on Highway 21, about two miles from downtown. A little further on Highway 170 at Cross Creek Shopping Center are Walmart and Penneys, about five miles from downtown.

🍄 **Hospitals**: Beaufort Memorial Hospital is located on Ribaut Road, about a mile and a half from downtown. The U.S. Naval Hospital is just a bit further down Ribaut Road, about three miles from downtown.

🍄 **Children's Playground Downtown**: In the waterfront park there's a playground with sandboxes, swings, jungle gyms and slides, all with a waterfront view and pleasant sea breezes.

🍄 **Public Rest Rooms Downtown**: These can be found in the waterfront park in the pavilion area.

🍄 **Where to Play Tennis Nearby**: Public tennis courts are located at the corner of Bladen and Boundary Streets, near downtown. Almost all of the golf courses (see below) also offer tennis.

GOLF COURSES

Although Hilton Head Island and its surroundings, about 30 miles from downtown Beaufort, are justly famous for golf, you needn't go that far for fabulous golfing. There are plenty of outstanding courses very near to downtown Beaufort. These are the closest ones:

🦌 **Brays Island Golf Course, 846-3100,** 18 holes designed by Ron Garl, is located on a working plantation at Sheldon, near the intersection of U.S. 17 with Interstate 95. Restricted to members, guests, and individuals interested in relocating to upscale Brays Island.

🦌 **Cat Island Golf Club, 524-0300,** 18 holes designed by George Cobb. Go across the downtown bridge, turn right onto Meridian Road, about six miles to Cat Island.

🦌 **Country Club of Beaufort at Pleasant Point, 522-1605,** 18 holes designed by Russell Breedon, located on Lady's Island, beautiful new clubhouse with restaurant and lounge.

🦌 **Country Club of Callawassie, 522-1533,** 27 holes designed by Tom Fazio, located just across the Broad River, 20 minutes from downtown Beaufort, off Highway 170.

🦌 **Dataw Island Golf Course, 838-8250,** 36 holes designed by Fazio and Hills. Dataw Island offers golf only to those interested in exploring Dataw Island's residential opportunities. Go across the downtown bridge straight ahead to St. Helena Island, left at the flashing light.

🦌 **Fripp Island Ocean Point Golf Links, 838-2309,** 18 holes on the ocean at Fripp Island. Go across the downtown bridge straight ahead to Fripp Island, about 18 miles. To play at Fripp, you must set up an appointment or you will not be allowed through the gate.

🦌 **Golf Professionals Club, 524-3635,** 36 holes, located on Lady's Island on Sam's Point Road (Route 802). Guest play is welcome on either the Champions or Players Course. Many northern visitors spend the winter months staying in their new guest accommodations.

❦ **Parris Island Golf Course, 525-2240,** 18 holes located on the Marine Corps Recruit Depot, is not just for the military, but also civilians as guests. Pictured in *National Geographic*, it may be the only golf course in the U.S. sitting atop an ongoing archaeological dig.

❦ **Tabby Links at Spring Island** is an 18-hole course designed by Arnold Palmer and Ed Seay, considered by many to be the finest course of Palmer's career. It includes tabby ruins of an old plantation. Play is restricted to members and their guests.

Fishing and Boating

The creeks, rivers and oceans surrounding the Sea Islands are renowned for onshore and offshore fishing. Shrimp, crab, oysters, clams, flounder, and numerous game fish abound including trout, redfish, cobia, tarpon, blue fish, and king and Spanish mackerel. Many fishing opportunities are available to satisfy serious and whimsical fishermen. The quickest and perhaps the easiest is to drop a line off the wall at the downtown waterfront park. The sides of numerous bridges also provide quick access to fishing "holes," especially at the Broad River Bridge out Highway 170 in the direction of Hilton Head Island and Savannah.

Because Beaufort is on the Intracoastal Waterway, we are host to sailors and boat travelers from all over the world. For those who are not familiar, the Intracoastal Waterway is a network of inlets, rivers, creeks and waterways along the coast that connect to form a water highway by which one may travel by boat all the way from

Maine to Texas without going out into the ocean. This waterway is especially pleasurable because of its numerous delightful ports and the protection afforded by river inlets.

Public ramps abound in our county where you may launch your trailer-borne boat. There is a ramp downtown at the end of the seawall by the downtown marina and a larger one immediately across the bridge on Lady's Island. If you are new to our waters, we urge you to consult tide and nautical charts and waterway guides before exploring. Our tides are extreme, shoals are everywhere, and the currents are treacherous at times. An ounce of prevention is worth a pound of cure.

FULL-SERVICE MARINAS

❦ **Downtown Marina of Beaufort**, located in the waterfront park, has overnight dockage with electricity, water, fuel, showers, laundry facilities, and a marina store. Outstanding overnight accommodations are right across the street at the Best Western Sea Island Inn for anyone desiring a night off the boat. Limited groceries are a block away at Blackstone's. Walk to all the downtown restaurants and shops. Be sure to monitor channel 16 as you enter Port Royal Sound from the south at the "2PR" buoy and follow the waterway 22 miles to downtown Beaufort. Or from the north enter St. Helena Sound and go 18 miles to downtown. The Downtown Marina is located at marker 239. There is plenty of deep water and the approach is easy, but be ready for fast currents.

🐚 **Port Royal Landing Marina,** located near the McTeer Bridge on the Beaufort River, has overnight dockage with electricity, water, fuel, showers, laundry facilities, and a marina store. There is an on-site bar and restaurant with good food and drink and a great chicken salad sandwich. Other restaurants and grocery stores are within walking distance. From the south enter Port Royal Sound at "2PR" buoy and follow the Intracoastal Waterway 20 miles. Or from the north enter St. Helena Sound and go 22 miles. This marina is located at marker 244. There is plenty of deep water and the approach is easy, but be ready for fast currents.

BOAT TOURS AND FISHING CHARTERS

One of the best ways to see the beauty of Beaufort is from the water. With the rivers and creeks literally defining our way of life, it would be a shame to miss this part of the Beaufort experience. Sunsets are especially gorgeous on the river here. There are many boat tours to choose from, but whatever you do, please call ahead to double check departure times and weather conditions. And don't forget your sunscreen.

❦ **Blackstone's River Tours of Beaufort, 524-4330,** docked at the Downtown Marina, offers sight-seeing cruises on a 28-foot pontoon boat. The tour lasts about 45 minutes. Refreshments from Blackstone's deli are available on request. This boat is a perfect size for small groups and families. Adults $10.50 and children $5.00. Call for departure times and information. Available for private charter.

❦ **Sea Wolf IV, 525-1174 or 525-6664,** is Captain Wally's sight-seeing tour boat departing from Port Royal Marina. Charters are available for deep-sea and gulf-stream fishing and diving offshore.

❦ **Sail Beaufort, 525-6852,** docked at the Downtown Marina. Expert sailor and licensed captain, Roger Marin, offers relaxing and informative sailing cruises aboard the beautiful Tripp-designed 40-foot Block Island sailboat named *Tribute.* Two-hour cruises cost $21.00 per person, refreshments included.

OVERNIGHT ACCOMMODATIONS

Downtown Beaufort is blessed with outstanding hostelries. You'll want to consider staying downtown because within walking distance will be the cream of Beaufort: historic houses and sites, specialty shopping, outstanding restaurants, the waterfront park, everything that makes the historic district of old Beaufort unique.

🦌 **Bay Street Inn, 601 Bay Street, 522-0050,** bed & breakfast at the east end of Bay Street on the water in historic and impressive Lewis Reeves Sams House, built in 1852.

Beaufort, S.C., November 4, 1882

Besides other attractions Beaufort has a first class hotel. The Sea Island Hotel has been thoroughly refitted with new furniture, new carpets, etc., and in every particular is up to the full standard. Suffice it to say that everything is new, with blending of colors and draping that has a most pleasant effect upon the eye even of those of the most cultivated taste.

—*Hotel Gazette*, New York City

🦌 **Best Western Sea Island Inn, 1015 Bay Street, 522-2090 or 1-800-528-1234,** is a modern inn with old-world features. Its 43 rooms have recently been thoroughly re-fitted with new furniture, new carpets, in every particular up to the full standard. The inn is complete with cable TV, meeting and banquet rooms, and private pool in a secluded courtyard. Located on the waterfront site of the historic Sea Island Hotel, this has been a hostelry location for almost 150 years.

❦ **Old Point Inn, 212 New Street, 524-3177,** a four-room bed & breakfast on the Point, is a cozy place to stay.

❦ **Rhett House Inn, 1009 Craven Street, 524-9030,** is a renowned, expensive bed & breakfast also offering fine dining on Friday and Saturday nights. In the historic Thomas Rhett House, built c. 1820.

❦ **TwoSuns Inn Bed & Breakfast, 1705 Bay Street, 522-1122.** This home overlooking Beaufort Bay was once called the "Teacherage" when it was a residence for school teachers in Beaufort. The five rooms are decorated in a variety of styles from Victorian to Oriental. ❧

Places to Live in and around Beaufort

MANY VISITORS who come to Beaufort are so enamored of the town that they decide to retire or have a second home in the area. You can fulfill your dream here—on the ocean, or overlooking the waterway, the vast expanses of marshland, a golf course, or woodlands of live oaks. Much of the property in and around Beaufort is on the waterfront or marsh, since the area is completely made up of islands. The following private communities are considered to be especially nice places to consider:

❦ **Brays Island**'s 5000 pristine acres of woodlands, pastures, ponds, and marshes is a sportsman's paradise. This exclusive, low-density community with golf, tennis, an equestrian center, indoor and outdoor swimming, and fine dining at an inn definitely appeals to the upper crust.

❦ **Callawassie Island** is a golfing paradise about 15 miles southwest of Beaufort. Tom Fazio designed the 27-hole golf course which takes up most of the recreational time of the residents. Golf fairways as well as homesites overlook the surrounding marshes.

❦ **Cane Island** is a small, quiet island about three miles from downtown Beaufort. The homesites are spacious with choices overlooking the Beaufort River and a pristine fresh water pond. No golfers or beachgoers here, just abundant, peaceful, undisturbed nature.

❦ **Cat Island.** This island is on the Beaufort River just past Cane Island. A George Cobb golf course is in the center of the island with homes and homesites along the waterfront, marsh and golf course.

❦ **Dataw Island** is a community of upscale homes and well-manicured lawns. A favorite of corporate retirees, Dataw has two golf courses (one designed by Tom Fazio), a marina, a large club house with an excellent restaurant, and miles of nature trails for biking and hiking.

❦ **Fripp Island.** It is almost impossible to stay indoors on a sunny day at Fripp. Beachcombers search the three and a half mile stretch of sand for shells and sand dollars. Golfers play 18 holes on the challenging seaside links course. Naturalists scan the marshes for birds, deer, small animals and plant life. And they all meet at sundown for drinks at the Beach Club pool where they decide which of the chef's specialties to try that night.

❦ **Newpoint,** across the river from Beaufort's historic district, is patterned after streets in old Beaufort. Residents can walk along the oak-lined sidewalks to visit with their neighbors or watch the sunset from the waterfront park and community dock.

❦ **Spring Island** will delight nature lovers and people who dream of owning an estate on an island. This island has one of the largest stands of live oaks on the East

Coast, as well as natural springs which feed fresh and salt water ponds and a waterfall. Quail hunting is a Spring Island tradition. Estate-sized homesites overlook the marsh, the river, and the newly-built Arnold Palmer golf course.

🦌 **The Village of Distant Island** is surrounded almost entirely by deep water, covered with live oaks and other mature trees, and located just a few minutes by car from downtown Beaufort. The island fronts on almost three miles of protected anchorages as deep as 23 feet at low tide. Looking due south toward the ocean, the island views the Intracoastal Waterway and Port Royal Sound, which can be reached in minutes by boats of all sizes. The Village of Distant Island is growing slowly and naturally as a small coastal village, like Beaufort in the old days—with true neighborhoods, tranquil streets, park benches, a fishing hole, bike racks, and tennis already in place.

Afterword

Frogmore, May 14, 1871

I do never intend to leave. I intend to end my days here and I wish to.

—Laura M. Towne

WELL, as you can see, Beautiful Beaufort By The Sea has a lot to offer. Some might think of Beaufort as a return to the past. Not so. Beaufort is very much a part of the late 20th century with the area having one of the youngest populations in the state.

Beaufort is a wonderful place to live. The people here are committed to making sure Beaufort will remain that way. This means being generous with praise for the values that make Beaufort special and skeptical of proposals that might threaten its uniqueness.

We like to think of Beaufort as a precursor of the future, an expression of the way people are supposed to live—in harmony with each other and with nature. So when you come here, either as visitor or settler, please remember to say a good word and smile. And do a good deed. In Beaufort, these characteristics are contagious.

Index

Coastal Villages Press is dedicated to helping
to preserve the timeless values of the old
villages along America's Atlantic coast—
building houses to endure through
the centuries; living in harmony
with the natural environment;
honoring history, culture,
family and friends—
and helping to
make
these
values
relevant
today.
This
book
was
completed on
March 21, 1994, at
Beaufort, South Carolina. It was
set in Caslon, used in the first printing
of the *Declaration of Independence* in 1776.